In a post-Christian age, th[...] apologetic resources has n[...] it could be argued that the task of apologetics has never been more pressing or more urgent. This is a critical time of cultural and intellectual transition. The Christian ministry, taken as a whole, must be understood as an apologetic calling. This is why books like *Why Should I Believe Christianity?* deserve careful reading by pastors and laypeople alike. In this book, believers will find a compelling defense of the Christian worldview and the resources necessary to stand firm in a faithless age.

R. Albert Mohler, Jr.
President of the Southern Baptist Theological Seminary
Louisville, Kentucky

James Anderson is one of the best writers in contemporary Reformed theology and apologetics. He has a wonderful gift for anticipating the questions in readers' minds and finding striking, appropriate illustrations. As in his previous book, he presents the Christian faith as a distinctive worldview. Within that worldview, there is no competition between presuppositions and evidences, epistemology and history. These cohere seamlessly, as God intended them to. This is one of the best sources available for presenting the rationale of the Christian faith to an unbelieving reader.

John M. Frame
Professor of Systematic Theology & Philosophy
Reformed Theological Seminary, Orlando, Florida

James Anderson writes with the mind of a scholar but the clarity and tone of a letter to a dear friend. His brief and engaging book covers a wide array of topics, from discussions on worldviews and evidence to philosophical arguments to inferences from the biblical record–all in the simplest terms possible. It can be read or given to anyone interested in an overview of the case for Christianity.

Brian Morley
Professor of Philosophy and Apologetics
The Master's College, Santa Clarita, California

If strong and persuasive arguments are going to be given against unbelief, at least two things have to be true of those arguments. First, they have to address the intellectual inconsistency of unbelief, in its myriad forms. Second, they have to be able to dive below the surface of objections to Christianity in order to crack the foundations of unbelieving thought. James Anderson does a masterful job of applying both of these, and thus of getting to the rebellious root of views that seek to oppose Christianity. This book will be a necessary tool for anyone interested in addressing arguments against Christian truth.

K. Scott Oliphint
Professor of Apologetics and Systematic Theology
Westminster Theological Seminary, Philadelphia, Pennsylvania

In a world filled with skepticism, relativism, and secular dogmatism, it is easy to doubt what we believe. Is Christianity really true? In this fantastic book, James Anderson offers one of the clearest and most compelling explanations for the truth of Christianity that I have ever read. You will be reassured and strengthened by this book. Read it multiple times. Then give it to a friend.

Michael J. Kruger
President and Professor of New Testament
Reformed Theological Seminary, Charlotte, North Carolina

The Big Ten:
Critical Questions Answered

Why Should I Believe

Christianity?

JAMES N. ANDERSON

SERIES EDITORS
JAMES N. ANDERSON AND GREG WELTY

James N. Anderson specializes in philosophical theology, religious epistemology, and Christian apologetics at Reformed Theological Seminary. He has also had experience serving in churches and is currently active in Ballantyne Presbyterian Church in Charlotte, North Carolina. He and his wife Catriona have three children.

Copyright © James N. Anderson 2016

paperback ISBN 978-1-78191-869-2
epub ISBN 978-1-78191-895-1
Mobi ISBN 978-1-78191-896-8

Published in 2016
by
Christian Focus Publications Ltd,
Geanies House, Fearn, Ross-shire
IV20 1TW, Scotland
www.christianfocus.com

Cover design by Paul Lewis

Printed by Bell and Bain, Glasgow

MIX
Paper from
responsible sources
FSC
www.fsc.org
FSC® C007785

CONTENTS

Dedication

To Eilidh, Erin and Luke:

Three proofs of God's existence

Acknowledgments

Heartfelt thanks are due to the following people who read an earlier draft of the manuscript and provided invaluable feedback: Catriona Anderson, Guillaume Bignon, Steve Hays, Nathan Johnson, Paul Manata, James Midwinter, Keith Plummer and Greg Welty. Any improvements in the final product can be credited to them; all remaining deficiencies should be blamed on me. I am also grateful to Stephen Greenhalgh for his excellent editorial work, and to the Board of Trustees of Reformed Theological Seminary for granting an eight-month sabbatical from my teaching duties in 2015, which enabled me to finish writing this book.

1

Introduction: Why Believe?

'I can't believe it. I simply can't believe it!'

It wasn't the first time Dr Campbell had encountered such a response from one of his patients, but on this occasion he had yet to discover quite how *literally* this particular patient meant it. Donald had just been told by Dr Campbell that he had been diagnosed with a very aggressive form of cancer that required immediate intensive treatment. Faced with this grim medical opinion, Donald simply refused to believe it.

'Sorry, Doc. I don't mean any disrespect. But I've never had a serious disease in my life. There's no history of cancer in my family. What's more, you need to understand that I have a wife, three children and a thriving career, and I've just been appointed chairman of the wine club. I simply can't *afford* to have cancer! No offence, but I'm going to get a second opinion.'

So Donald got a second opinion. And a third, and a fourth, and a fifth. Every doctor ran the same tests and came back with the same diagnosis as Dr Campbell. Nevertheless, Donald repeated his refrain to every physician he consulted: 'I can't believe it!' And he wasn't kidding. He really *didn't* believe it. He believed instead that all the tests must have been mistaken, and so he continued to live his life as though his body was entirely cancer-free.

The reality was that Donald *did* have cancer, just as Dr Campbell had first told him. He didn't believe Dr Campbell's diagnosis. But *should* he have believed it? If so, why? Before you answer that question, take a step back and consider this more general question: *Why should anyone believe anything?*

It's about Truth (and Reasons)

At the most fundamental level, we should believe things because they're *true*. Truth is ultimately what we're aiming for when we believe certain things and disbelieve other things. After all, no one thinks or says, 'I'm going to believe such-and-such, even though it's not true!' We recognize that our beliefs should be *true* beliefs rather than false beliefs. Ideally, Donald should have believed Dr Campbell's medical opinion because it was *true*. Whether or not his opinion was comforting, interesting, exciting, terrifying, or anything else—none of that was relevant to whether Donald should have *believed* it. Beliefs should be aimed at *truth*.

But of course, that's not the whole story. If I were to make some surprising claim—for example, that there are chess-playing chimpanzees—you'd be entirely within your rights to ask, 'Why should I believe that?' And if I were to reply, 'You should believe it because it's *true*', you'd be thoroughly underwhelmed by that answer!

The problem is that my answer doesn't tell you anything you didn't already know. When we ask, 'Why should I believe that?' we're really asking, 'Why should I believe that's *true*?' And what we're looking for are *reasons*: reasons to believe that it really is true. Reasons usually take the form of information, argumentation, or evidence that connects what we already know with what we don't (yet) believe to be true. So a better reply to your question would have been, 'You should believe it because I read a story about it in the *Daily Mail*.' (Depending on your view of the *Daily Mail*, you might need *further* reasons to believe it, but at least that would be a start.)

The point is this: while truth is *ultimately* what matters when it comes to beliefs, we often can't immediately determine whether our beliefs (or the beliefs of others) are true or not. Normally we have to rely on *reasons*— reasons that point us towards the truth, reasons that indicate whether our beliefs (or the beliefs of others) really are true. In the case of Donald's cancer diagnosis, he had very good reasons to believe what Dr Campbell had told him: the results of the various medical tests that had been performed, along with Dr Campbell's medical expertise and (we assume) his personal trustworthiness. The additional medical opinions Donald received gave him *further* good reasons to believe he had cancer. These served as *confirming* reasons. We can accept that Donald may also have had some reasons to *disbelieve* the diagnosis; for example, his previous good health and lack of any relevant family history. But in this case, as I'm sure you can appreciate, the reasons to believe considerably outweighed any reasons *not* to believe. Donald *should* have believed that he had cancer, no matter how psychologically or emotionally difficult it might have been to accept it.

WHY SHOULD I BELIEVE CHRISTIANITY?

This isn't a book about cancer, chimpanzees, or chess— at least, not directly. As you already know from the title, it's a book about Christianity.[1] But what we've just considered about beliefs, truth and reasons, is just as applicable to the question posed in the title of this book.

Why should you believe Christianity? Ultimately, I want to say, because it's *true*. In the final analysis, what really matters

---

1. I'll explain in more detail what I mean by 'Christianity' in chapter 3.

is whether the claims of Christianity are true—whether the world really is the way that Christianity says it is. For if Christianity really is true, that affects absolutely everything. The implications cannot be underestimated! As C. S. Lewis memorably put it, 'Christianity is a statement which, if false, is of *no* importance, and, if true, of infinite importance. The one thing it cannot be is moderately important.'[2]

But as we've seen, it's not nearly enough for me or anyone else to say, 'You should believe Christianity because it's *true*!' You should want to know what *reasons* there are to believe that Christianity is true. And that's entirely reasonable! So in this book I want to offer some basic reasons to believe that Christianity is true, as opposed to various other alternatives one might consider, such as Islam, Mormonism, Buddhism, Secular Humanism, Atheistic Darwinism, and so on.

Before we turn to consider those various reasons, however, it's important to clear away some common misunderstandings about the idea of truth—particularly the idea of *religious* truth.

'IT'S ALL RELATIVE!'

American academic Allan Bloom opened his bestselling book *The Closing of the American Mind* with these words:

---

2. C. S. Lewis, *God in the Dock: Essays on Theology and Ethics* (Eerdmans, 1972), p. 101.

'There is one thing a professor can be absolutely certain of: almost every student entering the university believes, or says he believes, that truth is relative.'[3] Professor Bloom made that statement nearly three decades ago, and, if anything, the view that all truth is relative is even more widespread today. As various surveys indicate, a majority of people believe that truth varies from person to person or from culture to culture. What's 'true' for one person or in one culture needn't be 'true' for everyone or in all cultures. There's no such thing as truth in any *absolute* or *universal* sense, relativists will insist. For such people, the idea that Christianity is 'true' wouldn't be enough for them to believe it. Christianity might be 'true' for *other* people, but that doesn't mean it has to be 'true' for them.

But is it really true that all truth is relative? (When the question is put that way, you can perhaps already see why the claim, 'All truth is relative', is very problematic.) There's a sense in which *some* truth-claims are person-relative ('Chocolate ice cream tastes great!') or culture-relative ('It's polite to shake hands when you first meet someone'). But the idea that *all* truth-claims are relative is actually quite irrational.

Take for example the claim that water has the chemical formula H_2O. Is that person-relative or culture-

---

3.   Allan Bloom, *The Closing of the American Mind* (Simon & Schuster, 1987), p. 25.

relative? Surely not. If it's true then it's an objective scientific fact, no matter who makes that claim or what their cultural background. Or consider the claim that the Japanese bombed Pearl Harbor in 1941. That's a true historical claim, because that's what actually happened on December 7th of that year. It's an objective historical truth. It isn't 'true' for some people but 'false' for others. It's just *true*—end of story. The same goes for countless other examples.

Not only is relativism implausible, it's also self-defeating. Just consider: Is the statement, 'All truth is relative', meant to be taken as true? Presumably those who make that claim think it's true. But if it's true, then what it says must apply to the claim itself. If *all* truth is relative, that has to include the truth that *all truth is relative*! It follows that relativism can be true for some people or cultures, but not for other people or cultures. But that makes no sense. How could truth be absolute for some people but relative for others? The problem is this: the claim that all truth is relative appears to be an *absolute* and *universal* claim about the nature of truth. But if it's that kind of claim, then the claim itself cannot be true after all. It's a *self-defeating* claim. It's as self-defeating as sawing off the branch you're sitting on.

At this point someone might say, 'Okay, I agree that some truth is objective. But religious claims aren't like scientific claims or historical claims. I think all *religious* truth is relative. Religion is basically about personal values, goals and lifestyle choices. And those are obviously person-relative or culture-relative. They aren't based on objective facts.'

Such a perspective is quite common in our day, but it's problematic on several levels. Its central flaw is that it's based on a false view of religion. It may be true that *some* religions are only about personal values, goals and lifestyle choices. But that's definitely not true for some of the major world religions. Christianity, Islam and Judaism all make significant *historical* claims about what took place in the past. For example, while Christianity and Islam take very different views of Jesus, both maintain that Jesus was a real historical person who lived in Palestine in the first century and performed miracles. If that's true, that's *objectively* true. Either there was such a person or there wasn't. Either He performed miracles or He didn't. Such claims can't be 'true' for some people but not 'true' for other people. They're questions of objective historical fact.[4]

---

4. Actually, the phrase 'true for me' is ambiguous. It might simply mean 'what I personally believe', in which case it would make sense to say, 'That's true for me but not for you.' However, that wouldn't be *relativism*. It would just be a recognition of the obvious fact that people have different beliefs. Religious relativism is the view that there are no objective facts, no objectively right answers, when it comes to matters of religion.

Let's take this a little further. One of the earliest Christian creeds, the Apostles' Creed, states that Jesus 'suffered under Pontius Pilate, was crucified, dead, and buried', and that 'the third day he rose again from the dead'. The claim that Jesus was executed by crucifixion but then rose from the dead has always been one of the defining claims of Christianity. Islam, on the other hand, denies that Jesus was crucified and resurrected. Could this central claim of Christianity be only *relatively* true? Could it be 'true' for some people (e.g. Christians) but not 'true' for other people (e.g. Muslims)?[5]

It's very hard to make sense of that idea—and that's certainly not how Christians and Muslims have understood their own beliefs. Whether or not Jesus was crucified is a matter of objective historical fact. Either He was or He wasn't. If that central claim of Christianity is true, it has to be true *period*—for everyone, everywhere, no matter who they are or what they happen to believe or feel about it. And the same applies if that central claim of Christianity *isn't* true.

In sum, while the claim that all religious truth is relative has a superficial plausibility, it doesn't stand up to

---

5. Again, this isn't about whether Christians and Muslims have *different beliefs*. Obviously they do! Rather, it's about which of those beliefs line up with what *actually* took place in first-century Palestine.

scrutiny when you consider the actual truth-claims made by the major world religions. Any particular religion, such as Islam or Christianity, could be true or it could be false. What it *can't* be is 'relatively true'—'true' for some people and 'false' for others, all at the same time!

'WHO CAN REALLY KNOW?'

Relativism is one way to dismiss religious truth-claims. Another way is *skepticism*. Whereas the relativist says, 'All religious truth-claims are relative', the skeptic says, 'Even if some religious claims are objectively true, no one can really *know* whether those claims are actually true.' Skeptics are *doubters*. They doubt that anyone can know whether any of the central claims of a religion are true.

I'm convinced not only that Christianity is *true*, but also that it's possible to *know* that Christianity is true. Bold as it may sound, I believe I know that the major claims of Christianity are true, and I believe that you, too—if you're open to considering them—can come to know that they are true. In the rest of this book I'll try to explain how that can be so. But at this juncture I want to say a few words about what it means to *know* something, to clear away a few more misunderstandings.

I often come across people who think that in order to know something you must have absolute, knock-down, drag-out, infallible, irrefutable certainty about it. If there's the slightest room for doubt about something—

the slimmest possibility of error—then you don't really know it. But if that were really so, we wouldn't know most of what we take for granted as knowledge. I think I know, for example, that I have a wife and three children. In theory, there's a remote possibility I'm wrong about that. Perhaps I'm the victim of an elaborate hoax along the lines of *The Truman Show* or I'm inside a virtual-reality simulation like *The Matrix*! But the mere possibility of being mistaken isn't a good reason to deny that I know what I think I know. Likewise, I know what I had for breakfast yesterday and where I parked my car this morning even though I *could* be wrong on both counts. You and I both know that Pearl Harbor was bombed in 1941, even though our knowledge is based on a chain of fallible human testimony.[6] You don't need to know something *infallibly* in order to know it.

What's more, it can be reasonable to believe something even if you wouldn't say you *know* it's true. For example, I wouldn't say I *know* that it will be sunny tomorrow, but based on the weather over the last few days, and the fact that three independent weather forecasters have made the same prediction, I think it's reasonable to believe that it will be sunny tomorrow.

---

6. In fact, almost everything we call 'general knowledge' is based on what we've been told by others: parents, teachers, textbooks, newspapers, websites, and so on, any of which *could* be mistaken.

Even if we don't know that some claim is true, we can still have good reasons to believe it. Think again of Donald's cancer diagnosis. We might not want to go so far as to say that Donald should have *known* that he had cancer after that first meeting with Dr Campbell, but at least we can say that Donald had good reasons—very strong reasons in fact—to believe that he had cancer.

You may have heard it suggested that we should approach everything with a 'healthy skepticism'. The idea is that our 'default' position should be one of *doubt* towards any beliefs or claims. One problem with such a stance is that it's self-defeating. You'd have to start by doubting the claim that we should start by doubting any claim! You'd also have to doubt other things that a 'healthy skepticism' has to take for granted: your sanity, your ability to reason, even your own existence. There's nothing healthy about that radical form of skepticism. Our goal shouldn't be to doubt whatever we can, but rather to examine our reasons for believing as we do.

As I stated earlier, I think you can *know* that Christianity is true. But even if I'm wrong about that, you can still have excellent reasons to believe that Christianity is true. And that's what this book is all about.

'YOU CAN'T HANDLE THE TRUTH!'

One of my favorite movies is the military-courtroom thriller *A Few Good Men*, which stars Tom Cruise as

Lieutenant Daniel Kaffee, a hotshot navy lawyer, and Jack Nicholson as Colonel Nathan Jessup, the intimidating commander of the U.S. Marine base at Guantanamo Bay. The story centers on the trial of two soldiers charged with 'conduct unbecoming of a Marine' because of their direct involvement in the death of a fellow Marine. In the climactic courtroom scene, Kaffee calls Jessup to the witness stand and questions him intensely about how the chain of command works on the base. Increasingly frustrated with Kaffee's dogged questioning, Jessup barks at him:

> 'You want answers?'
> 'I think I'm entitled to,' replies Kaffee.
> *'You want answers?'*
> 'I want the truth!'
> *'You can't handle the truth!'* explodes Jessup.

Nicholson's comeback has become one of the most quoted lines in movie history. In the context of the movie's storyline, the lesson is that there are difficult truths about how the military has to operate in some circumstances to protect our precious freedoms, truths that we would rather not know about or face up to. Yet the exchange between Kaffee and Jessup captures a more universal lesson about how fallible and flawed humans often relate to the truth.

On the one hand, many of us like to think we value the truth above all else. When it comes to any important issue of life, we put ourselves with Daniel Kaffee: 'I want the truth!' Whatever reality is, we want to *know* it. We don't want to live with false beliefs. We don't want to live a lie. Even so, one truth that's particularly difficult for us to accept is that the truth is sometimes too difficult for us to accept! Wouldn't it be wonderful if the truth always turned out to be the way we *want* it to be? Reassuring. Comforting. Not disruptive to our lives. Not demanding anything too strenuous from us. Not requiring us to make any radical changes to the way we approach the world. Yet sometimes, as our friend Donald discovered, the truth just isn't like that. And sometimes—like Donald and Lieutenant Kaffee—we can't handle the truth.

The reason I mention this is to drive home the main point of this opening chapter. Ultimately what we should be aiming for are *true* beliefs—not beliefs that are merely convenient, comforting, inoffensive, or self-affirming. And when it comes to believing Christianity, what matters above all else is *whether or not it's true*. If it really is true—and if we have strong reasons to think that it is true—then we should believe it. If it really isn't true—and if we have strong reasons to think that it isn't true—then we should believe something else.

No doubt some people believe Christianity simply because they *want* it to be true. They like what Christianity teaches. By the same token, there are people who *don't* believe Christianity simply because they *don't* want it to be true. Neither stance is intellectually responsible. The responsible approach is to consider the *reasons* for and against the *truth* of Christianity, and to draw the most reasonable conclusions we can. My hope is that this book will make a helpful contribution towards that end.

WHAT THIS BOOK DOES AND DOESN'T DO

As I draw this introductory chapter to a close, I want to be clear about what this book aims to accomplish and also what it *doesn't*. The title of the book is *Why Should I Believe Christianity?* and I want to give a basic answer to that question by offering what I think are some very good reasons to believe that Christianity is true. However, I also want to say some important things about *how* one should go about answering that momentous question.

One of the points I'll make in the next two chapters is that Christianity isn't merely a lifestyle, a moral code, a social identity, or a set of abstract theological doctrines. It's much more than any of those things. Christianity is an all-encompassing *worldview* and it needs to be understood and evaluated on that basis. Only once we assess Christianity as a distinctive worldview, alongside competing worldviews, will we be in a position to appreciate why anyone should believe it.

So my overarching goal is to explain, with minimal philosophical mumbo jumbo, what it means to say that Christianity is a worldview and why we should believe that it's the *correct* worldview. This book is a *summary introduction*. It isn't meant to be a comprehensive case for Christianity that goes into great detail on every point. However, at the end you'll find my recommendations for further reading on some of the important issues I discuss.

The other point to underscore is that this book doesn't directly address the various objections and criticisms that people level *against* Christianity (although I do touch on some of them along the way). As I explained earlier, if we're serious about considering the *truth* question—'Is Christianity true?'—then we ought to consider both reasons *for* and *against* believing that Christianity is true. This book focuses on the positive side of the truth question: reasons *for* believing Christianity. People have offered various reasons *against* believing Christianity: the problem of evil, apparent contradictions in the Bible, alleged conflicts between modern science and the Bible, the exclusivist claims of Christianity, the bad behavior of Christians throughout history, and so forth. These are all important issues, and they deserve a closer analysis than I can provide in a book like this. For that very reason, other books in this series will address such criticisms directly and in detail.

If that sounds a bit like a sales pitch, I suppose I have to admit that it is to some extent! Joking aside, however, my point is that this book isn't meant to stand alone. Be that as it may, I hope you'll find what follows helpful and thought-provoking as you consider for yourself the question, *Why should I believe Christianity?*

2

The Big Picture

Not long ago, my two daughters were given small toys by our local library as rewards for completing a reading challenge. The toys were called 'Puzzle Balls'. Each consisted of about ten oddly shaped plastic pieces of various colors, which had to be fitted together to make a perfect sphere. The girls tried all day without success to solve the puzzles. Their father, I'm ashamed to admit, did little better when he was summoned for assistance. Some of the pieces were T-shaped. Others were H-shaped. The rest were just bizarre. It was hard to believe they could actually be put together to make a sphere.

Only then did we pay attention to the little instruction sheet that came with the puzzles. We discovered that if we put the pieces together in a specific order, and in precisely the right ways, we could indeed make a perfect sphere. What's more, when the final piece was slotted into place the entire object locked itself tightly together so that it didn't simply fall apart when we put it down. It was an extremely satisfying moment!

I don't want to push the analogy too far, but there's a sense in which Christianity is like a Puzzle Ball. If you consider some of Christianity's distinctive teachings individually, in isolation from the whole, they can seem very hard to believe—quite outlandish, in fact. God made the universe out of nothing? God speaks to us today through a 2000-year-old book? God became a human being and died? A Jewish preacher came back from the dead—and then disappeared into the sky six weeks later? *Seriously*?

But just as you can't fairly judge a Puzzle Ball simply by looking at each of its individual parts on its own, so also you can't properly evaluate Christianity by considering each of its teachings in isolation. You have to put them together and examine Christianity *as an integrated whole*. When you do that, you discover that Christianity locks itself together in a very tight way. Its various claims explain and support one another so that they're tightly interwoven. Consequently, when each of its individual teachings is understood in light of the whole, Christianity makes excellent sense.

MORE THAN THE SUM OF THE PARTS

A couple of years ago, my family had the opportunity to visit the National Gallery in Washington, DC. My wife was particularly keen to see some of the paintings of the Impressionists such as Claude Monet and Edouard Manet. I'm no art critic, but I did discover that the best way to appreciate their paintings is to *stand well back*. You need to take in the whole work all at once to get the desired effect. If you stand up close to an Impressionist painting, it looks like a collection of rather careless, random brushstrokes. Only when you view those brushstrokes in the context of the whole picture can you truly appreciate the genius of the artist. The whole is more than the sum of the individual parts.

The same is true of Christianity. Some of its teachings, considered in isolation, apart from the context of the whole, seem to make little sense. In fact, trying to make sense of them in that way is like trying to interpret an individual sentence plucked at random from a novel, without any surrounding context or background information. My point here is a simple one, but often overlooked. If we're going to consider whether Christianity should be believed—whether Christianity is true and reasonable— we need to judge it *as a whole*, on its own terms, in its own context. As with so many things, Christianity is far more than the sum of its individual parts.

CHRISTIANITY IS A WORLDVIEW

One way to appreciate this point is to recognize that Christianity is a worldview, and therefore it needs to be *evaluated as a worldview*. Despite what many seem to think today, Christianity isn't something you can just clip onto your ordinary, everyday life like some kind of religious accessory. It isn't a Sunday pastime: churchgoing as an alternative to golfing or fishing. Christianity isn't merely a moral code, a social identity, a collection of religious traditions and practices, or a set of theological propositions—although it *includes* all of those things. No, Christianity is far more significant and wide-ranging in its depth and scope. Christianity is nothing less than a comprehensive, all-encompassing *worldview*.

But what exactly does that mean? In order to make the case for Christianity, I need to say a few things about what a worldview is and why it's important to think in terms of worldviews. Indeed, the topic of worldviews will take up the remainder of this chapter and play a central role in the following two chapters.

Let's begin with a basic definition of *worldview*. As the word itself suggests, a worldview is a comprehensive view of the world. I don't mean a *physical* view of the world, like the sight of planet Earth you might get from an orbiting space station. A worldview is a *philosophical* view of the world—and not just of our planet, but of the entire universe, indeed, all of reality. A worldview is an all-encompassing perspective on ourselves and everything else that exists, especially those things that matter most to us and have the greatest influence on our lives.

Our worldviews represent our most fundamental beliefs and assumptions about the universe we inhabit. They also incorporate and express our deepest values: what we see as the highest good, what standards we use to judge between right and wrong, what we value most in life and in other people, and what pursuits we consider most worthy. In sum, our worldviews reflect how we would answer all the 'big questions' of human existence: the fundamental questions we ask about life, the universe, and everything.

Is there a God? If so, what is God like and how do I relate to God? If there isn't a God, does it matter? What is truth? Can anyone really know the truth anyway? Where did the universe come from, and where is it going—if anywhere? Does my life have a purpose—and, if so, what is it? What does it mean to live a *good* life? Does it really matter in the end whether or not I live a good life? Is there life after death? Are humans basically just highly-evolved apes with superior hygiene and fashion sense—or is there more to us than that? Do we have inherent worth and dignity? What are our most fundamental rights and responsibilities?

Not everyone has considered all of these questions, let alone reflected deeply on them. But the answers you'd give to such questions, if you gave them some honest and careful thought, will expose your underlying worldview.

WHY WORLDVIEWS MATTER

Worldviews are like belly buttons. Everyone has one; we just don't talk about them very often. Or perhaps a better analogy would be to say that worldviews are like cerebellums. Everyone has one—in fact, you can't really live without one—but not everyone *knows* that he has one. Just as cerebellums are necessary for our *physical* lives, so worldviews are necessary for our *mental* lives. Each of us needs a worldview to bring some sense of order and understanding to the world we experience.

Have you ever watched a house being built? After the ground has been cleared, the first parts of the house to be built are the foundations and the framework. These parts are absolutely essential to the house. You can't have a house without those supporting structures. Worldviews have an analogous role in our thought-lives: they provide the foundation and the framework to the way we think about the world, the way we interpret our experiences, and the way we respond to those experiences. When we're living in a house, we don't often think about its foundations and framework, mainly because we don't *see* them. We're more interested in the immediate things: the décor, the furniture, the appliances, the upholstery, and so forth. But none of these other things would be possible without the foundation and the framework.

So it is with worldviews. We don't often think about our worldviews because they're usually in the background of our thinking about the world. Your worldview is the atmosphere of your thoughts. Like the air you breathe, your worldview is there all the time; you can't do without it, but you normally don't notice it because you're looking *through* it rather than *at* it. Without worldviews we wouldn't have any starting points for making sense of the universe we inhabit. Our worldviews reflect our most basic assumptions about what is real, what is possible, what is credible, what is reasonable, what is good and what is normal. Our worldviews typically include tacit assumptions about the nature, origin and destiny of the universe, as well as the nature, origin and destiny of human beings. What kind of creatures are we? Where did we come from, and where are we heading?

You can probably tell, then, that worldviews matter a great deal. Let me be more specific and give three reasons why worldviews are important. The first I've mentioned already: worldviews are *necessary* for our thinking about the world. Without some basic assumptions about what is real, what is possible, what is reasonable, and so forth, our thinking would be like an airplane without wings: it simply couldn't get off the ground. Our worldviews give a basic structure and stability to our thought-lives.

Secondly, worldviews matter because they greatly shape the way that we think about the world, ourselves, and our relationships with others. Indeed, your worldview is the single greatest influence on your thinking. How you interpret your experiences of the world, what conclusions you draw from those experiences, and how you respond to those experiences will be determined by your worldview more than anything else. Your worldview shapes and informs your experiences of the world. Like a pair of spectacles with colored lenses, it affects what you see and how you see it. Depending on the color and curvature of the lenses, you might see some things more easily, while other things will be de-emphasized or distorted. You might not see some things at all.

Let me illustrate with some examples. Suppose a close friend tells you that she recently met with a spiritualist who put her in touch with a loved one who died ten years ago. Later that same day, you read an article about a statue of the Virgin Mary that witnesses claim to have seen weeping blood. You also hear two news stories on the radio: one about possible signs of complex organic life discovered on Mars, and another about a father who killed his daughter (with the approval of the rest of his family) because she became pregnant out of wedlock, which is considered extremely shameful in their culture. How you interpret and react to those reports—and to everything else you encounter on that day, from the marvelous to the mundane—will be strongly influenced by your worldview: your background assumptions about God, the origin of the universe, human nature, life after death, our basic moral duties, and so forth.

Worldviews also largely determine people's opinions on matters of ethics and politics. What you think about abortion, euthanasia, same-sex relationships, public education, economic policy, foreign aid, the use of military force, environmentalism, animal rights, genetic enhancement, and almost any other major issue of the day depends on your underlying worldview more than anything else. Worldviews play a central and defining role in our lives.

Thirdly, worldviews matter because our worldview affects how we evaluate a truth-claim and how we interpret evidence for or against that truth-claim. Imagine you're speaking to a friend who believes in reincarnation. She believes that when people die, their souls are 'reborn' in other bodies (perhaps human bodies, perhaps not). When you ask her why she believes in reincarnation, she tells you that she has memories of her own past lives. For example, she remembers when she was a nurse during the American Civil War. In her own mind, that seems to be good evidence for reincarnation. But it's also likely that her worldview *predisposes* her to see that as good evidence. You, on the other hand, may have a very different worldview, a worldview in which reincarnation isn't possible (perhaps because you think humans are purely physical beings with no immaterial souls) or at least that it's highly unlikely. If that's the case, you'll tend to interpret her evidence—her supposed memories of past lives—in a way that better fits with your basic assumptions about life, death, human nature, and so forth.

The point here is that there's no simple relationship between worldviews and evidence. On the one hand, it's possible to evaluate worldviews on the basis of evidence. We can *test* our own worldview and the worldviews of others. On the other hand, how we *interpret* evidence (which can take many different forms) will largely depend on our worldview. So there's a complex two-way relationship between worldviews and evidence. And that means one can't refute another person's worldview simply by appealing to 'the evidence'. Evidence is just one part of a bigger picture when it comes to scrutinizing our own worldviews and those of others.

'THERE CAN BE ONLY ONE!'

If you're as old as I am, you may remember the classic movie *The Highlander* which starred Christopher Lambert as an immortal Scottish swordsman born in 1518 who has to battle other immortals throughout the centuries until only one is left alive. Perhaps the most memorable aspect of the movie was its tagline, repeated by several of its characters: 'There can be only one!' (The movie did have an answer to the obvious question—how do you kill someone who's immortal?—but whether it was a philosophically satisfying answer is a matter of debate.)

There can be only one! What goes for immortals also goes for worldviews, at least when it comes to the question of which worldview is *true*. It's tempting to think that it's merely a matter of personal choice what worldview you hold, or perhaps a matter of culture and upbringing. I see the world through my worldview, you see the world through your worldview, and there's no right or wrong about it. (The 'colored spectacles' analogy could be taken in this direction.) While it's true that our culture, upbringing and education do have a significant influence on our worldviews, we need to recognize a very important point: the fact that our worldviews are influenced by these factors doesn't mean that all worldviews are equally good.

The primary reason for this takes us back to our discussion of beliefs and truth in the first chapter. We should want our beliefs to be *true*, because true beliefs are better than false beliefs. Our worldviews involve beliefs, assumptions and value judgments, all of which can be true or false. So one worldview can be *more true* than another worldview, in the sense that it better represents reality. In that case, the first worldview is *better* than the second.

Let's consider a specific example. A person's beliefs and assumptions about God—whether there is a God, what God is like, how God relates to us, and so forth—play a major role in that person's worldview. Some people have a *theistic* worldview, which affirms that God exists (where God is understood to be the Creator of the universe). Other people have an *atheistic* worldview, which denies the existence of God. Clearly both can't be right. Either there is a God or there isn't. If there really is a God, then a theistic worldview is superior, simply because it more accurately reflects reality. Conversely, if God doesn't exist, then an atheistic worldview is much closer to the truth and therefore better than a theistic worldview.

Since different worldviews make conflicting claims and assumptions, they can't be *equally* true. Some worldviews are truer than other worldviews, and in principle there must be one worldview that is *most* true—a worldview that reflects the way things really are, better than any other worldview. So the all-important question is: *Which* worldview is that?

EVALUATING WORLDVIEWS

In the first chapter I explained that we should want our beliefs to be *true*, and the way we determine whether our beliefs (or other people's beliefs) are true is by considering *reasons* for and against those beliefs. The same principle can be applied to worldviews. We can consider various reasons for thinking that a worldview is true and also various reasons for thinking that a worldview is *not* true. Another way to put the point is to say that we can *evaluate* worldviews with respect to their truth-claims. We can apply certain *tests* to worldviews. In the remainder of this chapter, I want to suggest four tests that we can use to evaluate and compare worldviews.

The Consistency Test. This first test is simple to understand, but it's not always straightforward to apply in practice. Any worldview that involves inconsistent beliefs or assumptions cannot be true (at least at those points) because it's a basic rule of logic that no contradiction is true. Very rarely, however, will someone have a worldview that involves an *explicit* contradiction. I've never come across a worldview that says, for example, God both exists and doesn't exist!

What's more common is to encounter people with foundational convictions or assumptions that seem to be *implicitly* contradictory. For example, I've met people who think there are no moral absolutes—no moral laws that apply to everyone—but who also think there's a cosmic law of karma according to which we're rewarded for our good deeds and punished for our bad deeds (if not in this life then in the next). On the face of it these beliefs are inconsistent, because if there is such a law of karma, there must be absolute moral laws by which people's deeds can be judged 'good' or 'bad'. The lesson is that often we have to examine our worldviews more closely in order to see how internally consistent they are. To the extent that a worldview appears to be self-contradictory, we have reason to think that it isn't true. The caveat is that we need to make sure we've properly understood a worldview on its own terms before we accuse it of inconsistency.

The Coherence Test. This test is similar to the previous one, but it looks for more than mere logical consistency. The word *cohere* literally means 'to stick together' or 'to be united'. A worldview *coheres* if its parts hold together well and support one another. If a worldview includes beliefs and assumptions that appear to be unrelated to each other, or in tension with each other, then that worldview lacks coherence. Conversely, if a worldview includes beliefs and assumptions that are closely intertwined, where some parts explain other parts, then that worldview has coherence.

Here's a simple example of applying the coherence test. Suppose Katie believes that the universe was created by a personal God and also that there are objective moral laws which govern how human beings should live: laws that stand over us, which we didn't invent ourselves. Those two beliefs cohere well, because if we were created by a personal God, it makes sense to think that God designed us to live in certain ways—indeed, that God *wants* us to live in certain ways (e.g. respecting one another and not stealing from one another). Contrast Katie's worldview with that of her friend, Sam. Katie and Sam agree that there are objective moral laws by which we should live, but Sam has an atheistic worldview, according to which the human species is just a cosmic accident, a product of blind evolutionary processes with no ultimate design or purpose. On these two points—the existence of God and the nature of morality—Sam's worldview is less coherent than Katie's. For this very reason, many atheists have rejected the idea of objective moral laws. I think that's a serious mistake, but I have to give them credit for trying to maintain coherence in their worldview.

The Explanation Test. A good worldview will help us *explain* the things we observe about ourselves and the world we inhabit. As it turns out, some worldviews can better explain things than other worldviews—as philosophers say, they have more 'explanatory power'—which makes the explanation test a very valuable test for a worldview. If a worldview can explain things, and explain them well, that's a good indication that the worldview is true. If one worldview can better explain things than another worldview, we have more reason to believe the first than the second.

Once again, an illustration may help. Most people take for granted that there's something *special* about human beings. We treat other human beings with a moral respect and dignity that we don't extend to badgers or blowfish (to pick two species at random). According to some worldviews, such as Christianity and Judaism, human beings are special because we're created by God in His own image; in other words, we reflect the characteristics of God in a limited but unique way. So these worldviews offer a foundational explanation for why we ascribe special dignity to humans. In contrast, worldviews which assert that humans are the unintended product of blind evolutionary processes, along with every other organism on the planet, find it hard to give a good explanation for why *Homo sapiens* should be treated as more morally valuable, in any *objective* sense, than any other species.

The explanation test can be applied to many other things we take for granted in our everyday lives, such as the orderliness of the universe, the meaningfulness of human existence, and our ability to use reason to extend our knowledge of the world. You'll encounter further illustrations in subsequent chapters of this book.

The Evidence Test. This fourth test, like the first, is fairly easy to understand in principle but can be tricky to apply well in practice. The basic idea here is that if a worldview is true then it should fit with the evidence we have available to us: the immediate evidence of our senses, the evidence of reason, the evidence of conscience, the evidence of history, the evidence of science, and so forth. In the broadest sense, evidence is anything that can serve as a *truth-indicator*—anything that points towards the truthfulness of some belief or claim. The evidence we use in everyday situations is often observational in nature, based on sense perception, but it's important to recognize that direct sensory observations aren't the *only* kind of evidence. Our internal faculties of intuition, reason and conscience can also serve as sources of evidence for certain truth-claims. We rely on other external sources of evidence, too, such as the testimony of trustworthy people.

The evidence test is important because a person's worldview can be *confirmed* by the evidence or it can be *disconfirmed* by the evidence. That said, this test can be tricky because, as I noted earlier, there's a complex two-way relationship between worldviews and evidence. No one interprets evidence in isolation from their worldview. Since our worldviews include our ultimate presuppositions about what's real, what's reasonable, what's possible, and so on, our worldviews influence how we *interpret* any evidence that is presented to us. So we can't just point to 'the evidence' or 'the facts' to prove or disprove a worldview.

Nevertheless, evidence has an important role to play in our evaluation of worldviews, because some evidence has a better fit with some worldviews as opposed to others. If I were to pick an item of clothing at random from a store, the chances are that you'd be able to put it on *somehow*—but that doesn't mean it would be a good fit! Likewise, when presented with a piece of evidence, each of us will try to fit that evidence into our current worldview, but that evidence will fit better with some worldviews than with others.

One way to approach the evidence test is to consider what we'd *expect* to observe if a particular worldview were true. What would be surprising or unsurprising if that worldview were actually true? To take one example: the Christian worldview claims that the Bible is divinely inspired, which means that God guided the human authors to write what He wanted them to write. If that Christian claim is true, we'd expect the Bible to have some very special features, such as being consistent in its teaching, showing great insight into human nature and human problems, transforming people's lives, and revealing things that only God could know (such as making predictions about the future). If the Bible does indeed have those features, that's evidence *for* the Christian worldview—and if it doesn't, that's evidence *against* the Christian worldview. Certainly it would be surprising for the Bible to have those qualities if it were nothing more than a collection of flawed human writings.

The four tests I've outlined here aren't esoteric philosophical principles. They're really just common sense. They're tests that philosophers use to evaluate worldviews, but they're also tests that scientists use to evaluate theories and detectives use to evaluate hypotheses. In fact, we apply these tests as a matter of routine without really being aware of doing so.

There are other tests we could apply to worldviews that are more subjective or 'existential' in nature. For example, we might ask, 'Does this worldview give me a sense of meaning and purpose in life?' Or, 'Does this worldview give me comfort in the present and hope for the future?' Or, 'Does this worldview give me a sense of personal satisfaction and identity?' It's worth asking these kinds of questions too, and any worldview that can offer affirmative answers has something going for it. But we should also recognize that these questions aren't directly relevant to whether or not a worldview is *true*. Your worldview might include the conviction that everyone goes to heaven when they die, and heaven is a place where you get to do whatever you enjoy for eternity without any interference from others. Such beliefs might give you comfort and hope in the hard times, but that's no reason to think they're *true*. To answer the *truth* question, we need tests like the four I've outlined above.

Ideally, a worldview should be evaluated in comparison with *other* worldviews—at least with the major alternatives. The reason for this is that if we think a certain worldview faces some difficulty or problem, we might be tempted to dismiss it simply for that reason, without taking proper time to consider whether competing worldviews face the same or similar challenges—or perhaps even *greater* challenges. In other words, rather than asking, 'Which worldview passes all the tests without any problems whatsoever?' we should ask, 'Which worldview passes the tests better than any other worldview?' We will then be able to see which worldview is the *most reasonable* to believe. This worldview will be the one that is most consistent and coherent, that best explains the most important features of the world we inhabit and our experiences of it, and that can best account for all the evidence available to us.

One final observation before I wrap up this chapter. When evaluating worldviews, it's important to remember that each worldview should be evaluated on its own terms, not by the standards and expectations of *some other worldview*. Suppose you're comparing two worldviews: Worldview X and Worldview Y. If Worldview X is allowed to sit on the judge's bench when Worldview Y is on trial, it will hardly be surprising to find that Worldview Y is found guilty, simply because it isn't Worldview X. One might as well argue that the English language is flawed because it doesn't follow the grammatical rules of Latin. I emphasize this point because people who criticize Christianity often do so without realizing that their objections actually take for granted *some other worldview* than the Christian one. (This is particularly common when it comes to *moral* objections to Christianity.) In effect, the critics are judging Christianity on the basis of *non-Christian* standards and expectations. But that's rigging the deck in advance. Christianity needs to be evaluated on its own terms, like any other worldview. If it fails to live up to its own standards, so be it. But no one should reject Christianity simply because it isn't something other than Christianity.

3

Christianity as a Worldview

Recently I read about a survey conducted on an important political issue. The first question in the survey asked members of the public whether they agreed with a wide-ranging decision made by the U.S. Supreme Court. The majority of people gave a confident *Yes* or *No* in answer to that question. The same people were then asked to briefly explain the issue that the Supreme Court was asked to decide. Only a small minority of the people could give anything *close* to the right answer to the second question! The lesson should be clear: you can't properly evaluate something if you don't adequately understand the thing you're evaluating. Unfortunately, too many people are eager to register their opinions about things they know very little about.

The previous chapter made the point that Christianity is a comprehensive worldview, and therefore it needs to be evaluated *as a worldview*—ideally alongside the other major worldviews that people hold today. I explained what a worldview is and why it matters, and I summarised four truth-directed tests that we can use to evaluate worldviews. But in order to evaluate a worldview responsibly, we need to take the time to *understand* that worldview—and to understand it as an integrated whole. This book, of course, is about Christianity. So in this chapter I want to set out the central and defining tenets of the Christian worldview; that is, what the Christian worldview explicitly affirms and also what it takes for granted.

I should emphasize that my main purpose at this point isn't to give reasons to believe the Christian worldview (I'll get to those in due course). Rather my aim is simply to clarify the central claims of the Christian worldview. So I won't be directly applying the four tests I laid out in the previous chapter. Nevertheless, I want to encourage *you* to keep those tests in mind as you read this chapter. Start applying them right now!

Before I launch into an overview of the Christian worldview, you might well ask me, 'Why do *you* get to say what Christianity really is?' I'll be the first to admit, I have no special authority here. But I don't need to have any such authority, as long as there's *some* appropriate authority I can appeal to.

This raises a more basic question: Who gets to say what Christianity is or isn't? The short answer is to point out that Christianity is founded on the life and teachings of Jesus Christ, which are recorded in the Bible. From the very earliest times, Christians have taken the Bible as their foundational authority—in fact, they have taken it to be the Word of God. The Bible basically consists of two parts: the Old Testament, which was written before Jesus was born, and the New Testament, which was written by some of the earliest followers of Jesus. Jesus Himself treated the Old Testament scriptures as authoritative, going so far as to call them 'the word of God'. Moreover, He entrusted to His disciples the crucial task of testifying to His own life and teachings. Their testimonies are recorded in the New Testament. In short, Jesus believed the Bible was about *Him*, and He assumed that His followers would honor its teachings.[1]

---

1. See, for example, Matthew 15:1-9; 26:54, 56; Luke 22:37; 24:25-27, 44-47; John 5:39-47; 10:35; 13:18. For a fuller exposition of Jesus' view of the Bible, see John Wenham, *Christ and the Bible*, 3rd ed. (Wipf & Stock, 2009). Bible references such as 'John 3:16' refer to the Bible book called 'John', to the third chapter of that Bible book, and specifically to the sixteenth verse of that chapter. Thus, 'bookname xx:yy' refers to chapter xx, verse yy of bookname. Most versions of the Bible have a table of contents with page numbers to help you locate each book by name.

The upshot is that Christianity is founded on the Bible, and so the Christian worldview is none other than the worldview of the Bible, which is a worldview centered on Jesus Christ. So the overview of the Christian worldview I'm presenting here is really just a summary of the major teachings of the Bible. You'll see that I've provided a selection of references to specific verses or passages in the Bible to illustrate where these teachings can be found. My purpose in giving these references is not to say, 'You should believe this because the Bible teaches it', but rather to say, 'You can check for yourself that this is what the Bible—and, by implication, Christianity—actually teaches.'

IN THE BEGINNING ... GOD

Everyone enjoys a good story, and every worldview at some level tells a story. In fact, a good worldview ought to tell a *great* story—by which I mean not simply an enjoyable or interesting story, but a *grand* story: a story about *everything*. One of my eldest daughter's favorite subjects at school is history, and her main textbook has the title *The Story of the World*. As you can imagine, that's quite a long story! But there's a sense in which every worldview ought to tell 'the story of the world'. It should say something about where the world came from, how everything got started, which events and movements in history are the most significant, and where (if anywhere) everything is heading. Of course, different worldviews tell very different stories of the world. But there can be only one *true* story.

As every child knows, the best stories begin with the words, 'Once upon a time ...' In a sense, that's how the Christian story begins. The opening words of Genesis, the first book of the Bible, are: 'In the beginning ...' The story starts at the very beginning—a very good place to start! But this simple point shouldn't be overlooked. The Christian worldview has something very distinctive to say about how everything began.

So what exactly does Christianity say about the beginning of everything? The next word in the Bible is absolutely foundational:

'In the beginning, *God* ...'

At the very center of the Christian worldview is the presupposition that God is real and God is ultimate. God has existed from the very beginning, and God precedes everything else. The Christian worldview is an unashamedly *theocentric* worldview. It places God at the very center. Everything else derives its existence and meaning from God.

It's one thing to say that God exists. It's another to say what *kind* of God exists. What is God like? The

Bible, of course, has a great deal to say about God. All I can do here is to give an overview of the Christian understanding of God as presented in the Bible.

One way to summarize the biblical view of God is to say that God is both *absolute* and *personal*. To say that God is *absolute* is to say that nothing is more ultimate or foundational than God. God isn't defined or limited by anything else. God isn't dependent on anything else. On the contrary, everything else (as we will see in a moment) is dependent on God.

God doesn't exist because something else brought Him into existence. He isn't powerful because something else *made* Him powerful. He isn't wise because something else *made* Him wise. He isn't good because something else *made* Him good. God alone is the ultimate source of all existence, power, wisdom and goodness. And that means God is the final standard of all existence, power, wisdom and goodness. That's what it means for God to be absolute.

Not only is God *absolute*, He is also *personal*. The Bible always uses personal pronouns to refer to Him. God has personal characteristics: He thinks, He plans, He chooses, He speaks and He loves. Some religions teach that God is absolute, but not personal. According to those religions, God is not the kind of being with whom we could have a personal relationship. But the

Bible is clear: God is *both absolute and personal*. Like us, God is personal. Unlike us, God is absolute.

Another way to summarize the biblical view of God is to say that God is a *perfect* being, which means that He manifests *every perfection*. Every good characteristic a being could possess, God possesses to the maximum possible degree. God is perfect in *goodness*: there is no evil in Him. God is perfect in *knowledge* and *wisdom*: there is no ignorance in Him and He never makes mistakes. God is perfect in *power*: nothing is beyond His control, and He can accomplish whatever He wills. But whatever God wills, of course, must be perfectly good and perfectly wise. Nothing can defeat God's plans.[2]

Strictly speaking, the Christian worldview isn't alone in affirming that there is a God who is absolute, personal and perfect—although I would argue that only the Christian worldview *consistently* teaches that view of God. There is, however, one distinctive Christian teaching about God that is unique: the doctrine of the Trinity. According to Christianity, God isn't simply *personal*, He is *tri*-personal. There is only one God, but that one God exists eternally as three distinct persons, whom the Bible refers to as the Father, the Son and the

2. Deuteronomy 32:4; Psalm 145:17; Isaiah 6:3; 1 John 1:5; 4:7-8; James 1:13; 1 John 3:20; Psalm 139:4, 16; Isaiah 46:9-10; Romans 16:27; Isaiah 14:24-27; Matthew 19:26; Luke 1:37.

Holy Spirit.[3] These three divine persons exist eternally in perfect union and in perfect loving relationships with one another. The persons aren't *parts* of God—as though the Trinity were like a musical chord made by combining three individual notes—but rather each person is wholly God, somewhat analogous to the way that all three spatial dimensions of a solid object encompass the entire object.

The doctrine of the Trinity isn't explicit in the Old Testament, but there are strong hints of it throughout. For example, the writers speak of 'the Spirit of God' or 'the Spirit of the Lord' as a distinct personal agent who possesses divine power and authority.[4] These references to 'the Spirit' continue into the New Testament, where this divine person is referred to most commonly as 'the Holy Spirit'.[5] Furthermore, the Old Testament contains prophecies about a messianic figure who is sent by God but also equal with God.[6] So the Old Testament strongly affirms the unity of God, while also indicating plurality

---

3. Matthew 3:16-17; 28:19; John 14:16-17, 26; 2 Corinthians 13:14; Ephesians 4:4-6.

4. See, for example, Genesis 1:1-2; Judges 6:34; 2 Samuel 23:2; 1 Kings 22:24; 2 Chronicles 24:20; Ezekiel 11:1, 5, 24; Isaiah 11:2; 40:13.

5. See especially Acts 5:1-11.

6. Psalm 2:7, 12; 45:6-7; Isaiah 9:6-7; 61:1-2; Jeremiah 23:5-6; Daniel 7:13-14. We'll consider the divine nature of the Messiah in more detail in chapter 6.

within that unity. (The word *Trinity* is a contraction of *tri-unity*: it simply means 'three-in-one'.)

In the New Testament, the Christian view of the Trinity comes into clear focus with the coming of Jesus. Jesus claimed to be that messianic figure promised in the Old Testament. He referred to Himself as 'the Son', and spoke of His unique relationship with God as 'the Father'. Jesus taught things about His origins, power, authority and status which implied that He was equal with God. Indeed, His fellow Jews—who were strict monotheists—understood the implications of His teachings so well that they wanted Him executed for blasphemy.

The doctrine of the Trinity is clearly seen in two particularly striking incidents in the life of Jesus, as recorded in Matthew's Gospel. The first was at His baptism:

> As soon as Jesus was baptized, he went up out of the water. At that moment heaven was opened, and he saw the Spirit of God descending like a dove and alighting on him. And a voice from heaven said, 'This is my Son, whom I love; with him I am well pleased.'[7]

All three divine persons are present here: Jesus, the Son, is the one being baptized; the Holy Spirit descends on

---

7.   Matthew 3:16-17.

Him in the form of a dove; and the Father speaks from heaven, affirming the Son.

The second incident comes right at the end of Matthew's Gospel, where Jesus commissions His followers to take the good news about Him to the ends of the earth:

> Then Jesus came to them and said, 'All authority in heaven and on earth has been given to me. Therefore go and make disciples of all nations, baptizing them in the name of the Father and of the Son and of the Holy Spirit, and teaching them to obey everything I have commanded you. And surely I am with you always, to the very end of the age.'[8]

Not only does Jesus claim to have 'all authority in heaven and on earth', which His disciples would undoubtedly have understood as a claim to be equal with God, but He also explicitly identifies the three persons of the Trinity: the Father, the Son and the Holy Spirit. Strikingly, Jesus uses the singular *name* rather than the plural *names* to underscore the unity of the Trinity. There is one God, and thus one divine name shared by the Father, the Son and the Holy Spirit.

There's no question that the doctrine of the Trinity is mysterious. It is difficult—perhaps even impossible— for us to comprehend how one God can exist as three

---

8. Matthew 28:18-20.

distinct persons. Nevertheless, it is central to the Christian view of God. And despite its mysteriousness, it actually coheres very well with the idea that God is a perfect being. For if God is by nature perfect in every respect, He must manifest *perfect love*. But *other*-love, the love of one person expressed for another person, is a higher love than mere *self*-love. So God's perfect love must manifest a perfect form of *other*-love. In the beginning, however, there was only God! How then could God manifest a perfect *other*-love when all alone? The doctrine of the Trinity provides a profound answer to this conundrum: the Father, the Son and the Holy Spirit have always existed in perfect love relationships with one other. The Trinity, we might say, is the original perfect community.

HEAVEN AND EARTH

At the very heart of the Christian worldview, then, is the biblical view of God as the Absolute Being who exists in three distinct persons. So where do we fit into the picture? And how does our universe fit into the picture? The answers to these questions are provided by the Christian doctrine of *creation*.

To say that God is absolute is to say that He isn't dependent on anything else; rather, everything else depends on Him. God is eternal, which means that His divine life has no beginning and no end. He existed 'in the beginning', but that doesn't mean *God* began to exist. The universe, in contrast, is not eternal. As modern physics has confirmed, the universe hasn't been around forever. It had a beginning. So *how* did it come into being? Why does it exist at all?

For Christians, the logical answer is also the biblical answer: 'In the beginning, God created the heavens and the earth.' The phrase 'the heavens and the earth' translates a Hebrew expression which captures the idea of 'everything else that exists', or 'everything else that is real'. Everything that isn't God was created by God. Broadly speaking, the creation is divided into two realms: 'the heavens', the invisible spiritual realm, and 'the earth', the visible physical realm where we currently dwell.[9]

As you may be aware, Christians have taken different views about the details of creation. How long ago did God create the universe? Are the six 'creation days' in the book of Genesis meant to be taken as literal 24-hour days or are they figurative? Did God create every distinct species of plant and animal directly, or did He make basic *kinds* of creatures that could develop over time into

9. Sometimes in the Bible 'heaven' or 'the heavens' simply refers to the skies above the earth, where the birds fly and (much further out) the stars shine. But in other places those terms refer to a spiritual realm beyond the physical universe, invisible to our senses.

a variety of distinct species? Despite varying opinions on the details, the main contours of the Christian doctrine of creation are clear:

- God is the ultimate creator and sustainer of all things.
- God gave the universe the rational order and structure that it has (its natural laws).
- God is the author and sustainer of life.

Furthermore, God created everything *good* (because perfect goodness cannot create evil) and God created everything *for His own glory*.[10]

The Bible also has important things to say about how the Creator relates to His creation. Strikingly, the name most commonly used to refer to God in the Old Testament is 'the Lord'. Over and again we read about 'the Lord' or 'the Lord God'. This title is a very rich and weighty one, with several profound implications that are confirmed in other biblical teachings about God.[11] First, it implies that God has *absolute authority* over the entire creation. To put

---

10. Genesis 1:31; Psalm 19:1; Isaiah 43:7; Romans 11:36; Revelation 4:11. Of course, this immediately raises questions about the presence of evil in the world today. We'll come to that shortly!

11. My summary of God's 'lordship' over His creation is indebted to John M. Frame, *Salvation Belongs to the Lord* (P&R Publishing, 2006), pp. 3-14. Frame's book is an excellent introduction to the main teachings of the Bible about who God is and how we relate to Him.

it bluntly: God is the boss. God has the right to do as He pleases with His creation, and He has the right to tell His creatures how they should behave, simply because He is God. In short, *what God says, goes*. We should bear in mind, however, that what God asks of us will always be consistent with His perfect goodness and wisdom.

Secondly, 'the Lord' implies that God has *sovereign control* over the entire creation. Nothing in the universe is beyond God's ultimate control and direction. Nothing that takes place surprises God and none of it frustrates His plans for His creation. Everything that happens does so either because God brought it about or because He knowingly permitted it to happen. In short, *whatever God plans, happens*.

Thirdly, the lordship of God implies that He is *intimately and personally involved* with His creation. Some non-Christian worldviews present God as very distant and unknowable, like a divine absentee landlord. According to these worldviews, we can know that God exists, because there must be an eternal first cause, but other than getting everything started, God has little to do with the universe. The Christian view is vastly different. Just as a good king will make his presence known throughout his kingdom, and will engage personally with his citizens, so 'the Lord' makes His presence known throughout His creation and He engages personally with His creatures—especially with those He created 'in His own image'.

And that brings us to the next component of the Christian worldview: its view of mankind.

A Little Lower Than the Angels

Just as every worldview has something to say about God, so too every worldview has something to say about mankind: what kind of beings we are, where we came from, what our purpose is, how we're meant to live, and where we're heading. Since the Christian worldview has such a distinctive view of God, it's not surprising that it also has a very distinctive view of mankind, one with profound and wide-ranging implications.

If God created all things, that must include humans. But it also includes meteors, oak trees, earthworms and rabbits. So what's special about us? One of the most precious elements of the Christian worldview is expressed in the first chapter of Genesis:

> So God created mankind in his own image, in the image of God he created them; male and female he created them.[12]

According to the Bible, we're created beings—of course—but unlike other living creatures we're made 'in the image of God'. In a unique way, we reflect some of the characteristics of our Creator. We're *personal* beings.

---

12. Genesis 1:27.

We can think and reason. We can make plans and choices. We can experience and express emotions. We understand the distinction between good and evil, and we can make moral judgments. Most wonderfully of all, we're capable of *love*. We can know the joy of both giving and receiving love from another person. In all of this, we reflect in a limited fashion the inner life of the Trinity.

The biblical view that humans are created in the image of God implies that we have great worth and intrinsic dignity, such that we must treat one another with deep respect. It also indicates weighty *responsibilities* on our part. As the book of Genesis teaches, while God is the ultimate Lord of the universe, He has delegated to us the responsibility of ruling over the creation: a rule that implies care and nurture for what God has made, rather than a licence to domineer and exploit. We are God's deputies on earth.[13]

Another vital element of the Christian worldview is that men and women are *equally* created in the image of God. While men and women are obviously different in significant respects, God designed the two genders to complement one another. Nowhere is this seen more vividly than in marriage, the foundation for family life, which serves in turn as the basic building-block of human societies. In the Christian view, marriage is

---

13. See Genesis 1:28 and Psalm 8:5-8 (from which the title of this section is taken).

both a divine gift and a divine institution. Marriage isn't a universal obligation, but it is the normal expectation, simply because it's the God-ordained means by which men and women may enjoy loving companionship, sexual intimacy, and the opportunity to have children and thereby extend the human race from generation to generation. All this reflects God's basic design for human society. The plurality-in-unity of the human family, and the broader human community, is a creaturely reflection of the plurality-in-unity of the Trinity.

One question every worldview addresses at some level is this: *Why are we here?* Or posed another way: *What is our ultimate purpose?* Some worldviews offer a very depressing answer: 'There's no reason and no ultimate purpose.' In contrast, the Christian worldview offers a supremely positive and motivating answer to that basic question. It can be stated in various ways, but one classic summary statement comes from a seventeenth-century Christian document known as the Westminster Shorter Catechism: 'The ultimate purpose of mankind is to glorify God and to enjoy Him forever.'[14]

In terms of a Christian worldview, the rationale for that answer isn't difficult to discern. Since God is our creator, and perfect in every way, He is supremely worthy

---

14. I've paraphrased the original, which reads: 'Man's chief end is to glorify God, and to enjoy him forever.'

of our praise and worship. God didn't *have* to create us, but He freely chose to do so as an expression of His power and goodness. What's more, God delights to share His own inner life with us. While we can experience great happiness in our relationships with our fellow human beings, nothing can remotely compare with the delight of knowing the love of God. So our highest goal, as creatures made in the image of God, must be to reflect the glory of God and to enjoy the goodness of God without hindrance, without interruption, and without end. Knowing God in all His glory is our greatest good and our highest goal. How could it be otherwise?

REBELS WITHOUT A HOPE

Consider what we've covered up to this point. At the foundation of the Christian worldview is the conviction that the universe is the creation of an absolute, personal, perfect God. God made the universe, and He made it good. What's more, God created *us* in His own likeness. But clearly that's at odds with the world as we find it today. There are countless things in the universe that *aren't* good. And there are countless things about *us* that aren't good. So isn't the Christian worldview proven false right from the very start? Isn't it dead on arrival? Not at all. For Christianity affirms not only a doctrine of creation, but also a doctrine of 'the fall'. Both of these need to be affirmed together in order to make sense of the world as we know it today—and to make sense of the *rest* of the Christian worldview.

Although I currently live in the United States, I'm British by birth. One of the great attractions of Great Britain, besides its world-renowned cuisine and dental hygiene, is its long and fascinating history, much of which can be appreciated from the monuments and other architecture scattered across its landscape. Of particular interest are the many castles one can visit, some of which date back as far as the eleventh century. These fortified buildings would have been magnificent constructions in their day, but most of them now lie in ruins as a result of enemy attacks or the relentless forces of nature.

One might say that from a Christian perspective our world is a ruined castle on a cosmic scale. It was once magnificent, and it still shows signs of its greatness, even though it has been corrupted and spoiled. But how did this happen? The short answer: *It's our fault*. According to the Bible, the world is in the state it's in because we've messed it up. We haven't lived the way God intended us to live, and the consequences have been absolutely dire. Instead of following the way of goodness, truth and beauty, we've pursued wickedness, falsehood and ugliness instead.

Great tomes have been written on the Christian view of the fall of mankind, and Christians have disagreed over some of the details, but the outlines of the biblical story are clear enough. Adam and Eve, the first human couple, were created to live in perfect loving fellowship with God and with each another. In order to do so, they had to observe the laws laid down by their Creator: laws that acknowledged their proper place in the world and the distinction between good and evil, between godliness and ungodliness. In this basic duty, they failed. While they had the capacity to obey God's laws, they also had the capacity to disobey—that is to say, they had the freedom to choose between good and evil—and for reasons we may never understand they chose to go their own way rather than follow the way of blessing set out for them. They committed high treason against the King.

This act of cosmic treason was catastrophic for the human race and for the world at large. Its consequences can be captured in three words: *condemnation*, *corruption* and *curse*. In the first place, the fall brought *condemnation* on all mankind. According to the Bible, Adam was 'Everyman'. He represented the entire human race, such that when he rebelled against God, it wasn't just one man's rebellion: it was *mankind's* rebellion.[15] Precisely

15. In Hebrew, the name *Adam* is the same as the word for *mankind*. The most direct statements about the connection between Adam's rebellion and ours can be found in Romans 5:12-21 and 1 Corinthians 5:21-22. See also Romans 1:18-32 for a summation of mankind's rebellion against God and its consequences.

because God is absolutely pure in His goodness and justice—what the Bible calls God's *holiness*—our rebellion alienated us from Him and brought us under His righteous judgment. The original perfect love relationship was broken; now in its place we experience guilt, fear and resentment.

Secondly, the fall brought *corruption* to the human race. Not only did Adam spoil his relationship with God, he spoiled himself and all of his descendants. Human nature became stained with sin, so that we are all born rebels by nature.[16] Our hearts are inclined towards our own selfish interests, rather than toward God. It doesn't come naturally to us to love God and our fellow human beings. Instead, selfishness and conflict are the natural fruit of the human heart.

Thirdly, the fall brought a *curse* on the world: a curse inflicted on the creation by the Creator Himself as part of the penalty for human sin and a continual reminder of our predicament.[17] God's original design was that we would live in harmony with one another and with our environment. But now we experience alienation:

---

16. Genesis 6:11-12; Jeremiah 17:9; Matthew 7:11; Mark 7:20-23; Romans 3:10-18. The concept of 'sin' in the Bible encompasses not only specific moral violations against God and against one another (e.g. 'the sin of idolatry') but also our general state of moral corruption.

17. Genesis 3:16-19; Romans 8:18-25.

from God, from each other, and from the natural world around us. Life is hard. For most people, it's horribly hard. It's a continual struggle for survival. There is sickness, poverty and war. We're constantly threatened by natural disasters such as earthquakes, hurricanes, floods, diseases and famines. Our world bears all the marks of a creation that was originally good but now is horribly broken.

For mankind the most painful and humiliating element of the fall is *death*. Death encompasses all three aspects of the fall: condemnation, corruption and curse. According to the biblical worldview, human life has both a *physical* aspect (pertaining to our bodies) and a *spiritual* aspect (pertaining to our souls). Death is nothing less than the negation of life. Death isn't cessation of existence, as in many non-Christian worldviews, but rather a state of separation from the source and author of life.[18] Our rebellion against God has separated us from Him, like a lake cut off from the streams of fresh water that feed it. Such is the fate of those who turn their backs on their Creator.

Commenting on the Christian view of the fall and its consequences, the writer G. K. Chesterton said that it is 'the only part of Christian theology that can really be proved.'[19]

---

18. Isaiah 59:2; Romans 6:23; Ephesians 4:18.

19. G. K. Chesterton, *Orthodoxy* (John Lane Company, 1908), p. 24.

His point was that of all the elements of a Christian worldview, this is the one that our immediate experience readily confirms. One only has to switch on the television or browse a social media website to find the evidence on full display. In the week that I write this, the news is dominated by the latest outbreak of conflict in the Middle East, acts of stomach-turning savagery by Islamic militants in Iraq and Syria, and a series of riots and looting sprees triggered by the shooting of a teenager by a police officer in an American town. No doubt these stories will drop out of the headlines in due course, but one thing is certain: they'll be replaced by other stories no less distressing.

One recent news report particularly illustrates the depravity of which humans are capable. An Australian father took his three young sons to Syria to fight in an Islamic jihad. As if that weren't bad enough, he posted on social media a photograph of his seven-year-old holding up the severed head of a Syrian soldier with the caption, 'That's my boy!' Such examples represent the extremes of human wickedness. But before we console ourselves with our own relative righteousness, we should remind ourselves that most of those who participated in the Nazi concentration camps were otherwise 'ordinary' people. Even those who didn't actively participate turned a blind eye to the atrocities; they perversely rationalized their failure to protest. Nazism was supported by hundreds of thousands of 'civilized' Europeans. One of the least welcome lessons of twentieth-century history—indeed of all human history—is that once social taboos and the threat of punishment are removed, virtually *anyone* is capable of atrocities when their own comfort and survival is at stake. Malcolm Muggeridge hit the nail on the head: 'The depravity of man is at once the most empirically verifiable reality but at the same time the most intellectually resisted fact.'

According to the Christian worldview, then, we are tragically fallen creatures. From our earliest years our hearts are inclined toward evil, and all of us are capable of great wickedness. Even when we act respectably, we do so with mixed motives and impure hearts. And the worst part of it is this: *We cannot fix ourselves*. Both morally and spiritually, we have dug a deep pit and jumped into it, and now we cannot climb out.

GOD SPEAKS

If that were the end of the Christian story, it would be a pretty rotten one, and I certainly wouldn't have bothered to write this book. But in order to grasp the *good* news—what the Bible calls 'the gospel'—we need to understand the *bad* news with which it contrasts. Furthermore, before we get to that good news, we need to appreciate another defining element of the Christian worldview: the God who made the universe is also a God who *speaks*.

The influential Christian writer Francis Schaeffer encapsulated this idea in the title of one of his books: *He Is There and He Is Not Silent*. In contrast to the worldview of Deism, which affirms a transcendent creator but denies that this deity personally interacts with its creation, the Christian worldview affirms not only that God is intimately involved in His creation but also that He relates to us by *speaking* to us. This really shouldn't be surprising given that God has created us as personal beings with the power to express complex thoughts through language. Our capacity for language is one of the most distinctive and valuable features of human beings. It's one of the capacities that set us apart from every other living organism. So if our Creator is going to relate to us in a personal way, by communicating to us important truths about our relationship to Him and to one another, it makes perfect sense that He would do it through *language*, because that's how we normally communicate truths. How else would it be done?

The Bible acknowledges that God has spoken to human beings in various ways through the ages.[20] Originally, so it seems, God spoke directly to the first man

---

20. Hebrews 1:1.

and woman by appearing to them in an angelic form.[21] This mode of communication continued on occasion following the fall of mankind.[22] God also spoke to people through dreams and visions.[23] His most common way of speaking, however, was through divinely inspired prophets who served as intermediaries between God and His people. Sometimes the prophets brought messages of guidance or instruction, sometimes messages of warning or judgment, and sometimes messages of hope and promise. A central tenet of the Christian worldview, then, is that God has communicated through divinely appointed prophets who have authority to speak 'the word of God' to their fellow humans.

The Bible identifies quite a number of prophets, some of whom are well-known: Abraham, Moses, Elijah and Jonah, for example. But the most famous prophet of all is the central figure of Christianity: Jesus Christ. Of course, Christians believe that Jesus was much *more* than a prophet. But He was certainly no less than one. Indeed, Jesus is viewed as the pre-eminent prophet of God, because He wasn't merely an intermediary between God and humans.

---

21. Genesis 3:8.

22. Some examples: Genesis 16:7-14; 18:1-8; Numbers 22:31-35; Judges 6:11-24.

23. Some examples: Genesis 15:1; 20:3; 31:11; Numbers 12:6; Isaiah 6:1-11; Joel 2:28; Nahum 1:1; Matthew 1:20; 2:13; Acts 9:10; 18:9.

The startling claim of Christianity is that Jesus was none other than *God speaking to us directly in human form*.

But we're getting ahead of ourselves. I'll return to the idea of Jesus' divinity in just a moment. For now I just want to make the connection between the idea that God speaks and the Christian view of the Bible. The simplest way to put it is to say that the Bible is a collection of divinely inspired prophecies: words from God, given through prophets, which have been written down and preserved as 'inspired scriptures'. The Old Testament contains prophecies that pre-date the birth of Jesus. The New Testament contains the teachings of Jesus Himself, as well as the teachings of His apostles. (The apostles were Jesus' closest disciples, whom He appointed to bear witness on His behalf after He departed.) That's why Christians call the Bible 'the word of God'. Even though it's comprised of human words—it has to be in order for us to understand it—God spoke *through* its human authors so that their words are ultimately *God's* words. And because we still have the Bible today, God *continues* to speak to people through its words.

So another key element of the Christian worldview is the conviction that God speaks. But what does God say? The full answer is found in the Bible itself—from Genesis to Revelation. The briefer answer is that God speaks to us about three major topics:

- God speaks about *God*: who He is, and how He interacts with His creation.

- God speaks about *us*: what He made us to be and to do, and what we have actually done and become.

- God speaks about *salvation*: what He has done—and will do—to get us out of the mess we've made for ourselves.

And that brings us directly to the next major element of the Christian worldview.

GOD SAVES

Salvation. The word is a staple of Christian literature, not to mention the Bible. Christianity can hardly be defined without it. But there's a sense in which any worldview, even a secular one, needs to speak about 'salvation', whether or not that exact word is used. For any worldview worth its salt should reflect some idea about what's wrong with the world and how it needs to be put right: some idea of the basic human problem and the solution to that problem. The Christian worldview is no exception; indeed, its understanding of salvation is situated center stage.

We've already covered the Christian view of what's wrong with the world. We've rebelled against our Creator, bringing condemnation and corruption upon ourselves, and a curse upon the entire creation.

But there's one aspect of the human predicament that makes it particularly tragic and intractable. Not only have we made a mess of ourselves and of the world, our corrupted state means *we cannot fix the problem ourselves*. Because we're fundamentally broken creatures, polluted in our very natures, we're no more able to fix ourselves than we're capable of lifting ourselves off the ground by pulling on our shoelaces. A patient who's in critical condition, on life-support, can't serve as his own doctor. A similar principle applies in the spiritual realm. On the Christian view, our sin has alienated us from God, but anything we might do to remove that alienation, by trying to make amends with God, will be polluted with further sin.[24] You can't purify dirty water by filtering it through soiled sheets!

Our one and only hope is for our Creator to step in and save us. And the astonishing message of the Bible is that despite our rebellion against our Creator, despite the fact that God is absolutely pure in His goodness, and our sin is infinitely offensive to Him, *God has indeed stepped in to save us*. The biblical term for this message is 'the gospel', which literally means 'good news'. The bad news is that we desperately need to be saved, but we cannot begin to save ourselves. The good news is that *God saves*.

---

24. Isaiah 59:1-8; 64:6-7.

And it isn't a last-minute, I-suppose-I'd-better-step-in-and-fix-things kind of salvation. Because of His immeasurable love and mercy, God planned our salvation *from the very beginning*, before any of us asked for it or even realized that we needed it—indeed, before any of us ever existed. God took the initiative in our salvation, because He *had* to take the initiative. Had it been up to us, we would have been forever lost.

So what exactly has God done to save us? The Christian view can be summarized in three weighty words that require some unpacking: *incarnation*, *atonement* and *resurrection*.

In the first place, God became *incarnate*, which means that He took on a human nature and became a flesh-and-blood human being. To be precise, God the Son—the second person of the Trinity—became the God-man, Jesus of Nazareth. He became fully human, born to an ordinary woman in an extraordinary way, all without giving up His divine nature. He didn't change from being God to being merely a man, like some kind of metaphysical downgrade. Rather, He became *both God and man*. He did this in part so that He could identify with us, by becoming one of us and living with us in our fallen world. But the deeper reason is that in order to execute His plan to save us from our sin He *had* to become human.

That takes us to the second word: *atonement*. One consistent theme in the Old Testament is that human sin is a very serious matter before God, and every sin demands a penalty to be paid. The entire system of animal sacrifices was intended to reinforce that principle, as the Old Testament book of Leviticus made clear. Since God is the author of life, to rebel against God is to forfeit one's life: the ultimate penalty for sin is *death*. In order to escape that penalty, a fitting atonement has to be made. No animal sacrifice could really make atonement for human sin. Only a human sacrifice could accomplish that. But as I noted above, no *sinful* human could serve as an adequate atonement. Only a perfect, sinless human could make a satisfactory atonement before God, by offering up His own life to pay the just penalty for human sin. And that's exactly what the God-man did.

The Christian doctrine of atonement can be boiled down to four words: *Christ died for us*.[25] Jesus Christ, the God-man, lived the perfect life that we had failed to live, and He laid down that perfect life to make atonement for us. When He suffered an agonizing death by crucifixion, He bore the penalty for our sins in our place. He freely volunteered to take upon Himself the condemnation we deserve, so that we might escape that condemnation

---

25. Romans 5:8.

and be reconciled with the Creator who made us and still loves us.[26] We are treated as sinless and righteous in God's sight, not because of anything we have done but because of everything Jesus has done.[27]

But the death of Christ, while necessary for our salvation, wasn't the last word. If Christ had stayed dead, a question mark would have forever hung over the atonement. Did it succeed? Did it accomplish our salvation? Does death have the final word? Far from it! For the atonement of Christ is brought to completion by the *resurrection* of Christ. This is another defining tenet of the Christian worldview: Christ not only died for our sins, but also rose from the dead three days later.[28] Jesus' resurrection was a fulfilment of Old Testament prophecy, a vindication of what He had taught about His identity and His mission, and a foretaste of the final destiny of those He came to save.

So the good news of Christianity is that *God saves sinners*—and He saves us through the incarnation, atonement and resurrection of Jesus Christ. Does that mean every sinner will be saved? Much as we might want that to be true, it doesn't logically follow. On the one hand, Christianity teaches that salvation is a free gift

---

26. Romans 3:21-26; 8:1-4.

27. Romans 4:1-8; 2 Corinthians 5:21; Titus 3:4-7.

28. Acts 2:22-24; Romans 4:25; 1 Corinthians 15:1-8.

of God: it cannot be earned by anything we do.[29] But like any freely offered gift, the gift of salvation must be received and not refused. It must be accepted in the right spirit. And the New Testament makes clear that only two things are needed for the gift of salvation to be received: *faith* and *repentance*.

Whenever Jesus or His apostles were asked what one must do to be saved, the two answers that come up consistently are 'repent of your sin' and 'have faith in Jesus' (or 'believe in Jesus').[30] But what exactly does that involve? Let's start with the idea of faith. Critics of Christianity have often characterized faith as 'believing without evidence'—or worse still, 'believing against the evidence'!

In the context of the Christian worldview, however, that's not at all what faith means. The biblical idea of faith is simply the idea of *trust in a person*.[31] Trusting people is one of the most natural things in the world. We trust people all the time: our parents, our spouses, our teachers, our colleagues, our teammates, and so on. And the trust we put in people isn't a *blind* faith. It's usually a trust based on what we *know* about those people. The same basic idea applies to faith in Jesus. To have faith

---

29. Romans 4:4-5; 6:23; Ephesians 2:8-9.
30. Acts 2:38; 3:19; 10:43; 13:39; 16:31; 17:30; 18:8; 20:21; 26:20.
31. In the New Testament, the same Greek word (*pistis*) is used for belief, faith and trust.

in Jesus is simply to *trust in Jesus*: specifically, to trust that He is who He claimed to be, that He did what He claimed to do, and that He is able to save us completely from our sin and its deadly consequences. Christians trust Jesus for their salvation because they have good reason to believe He is a *trustworthy* savior.

What about repentance? In a sense, repentance is just the other side of the coin of faith. Faith involves *turning toward something*—or rather, toward *someone*: Jesus Christ. Repentance involves *turning away from something*: our sin and rebellion against God. It means confessing that we're sinners and renouncing our former way of life, a self-centered rather than God-centered way of life, and committing ourselves to follow the way of Christ instead. It's crucial to understand that the requirement to repent *doesn't* mean we have to clean up our lives before we can be saved. If we could do that ourselves, we wouldn't need to be saved in the first place! Rather, repentance is the expression of a sincere change of heart. It's a recognition that we have utterly failed to love God and others as we should, a sense of deep sorrow at our sinfulness, and a plea to God for mercy and forgiveness.

The Meaning of Salvation

We've considered the Christian view of why we need to be saved, what God has done in order to save us, and what we need to do to receive that salvation. But what exactly does it mean to be 'saved'? What difference does salvation make? Literally millions of pages have been penned by Christian theologians on what salvation involves, but to spare your patience I'm going to boil it down to three simple points.

First, salvation means *forgiveness*. When we repent and trust in Christ, all of our sins—past, present and future—are fully and finally pardoned, because Christ paid the penalty for every one of them through His sacrificial death. Forgiveness means that the guilt of our wrongdoing is removed and the threat of divine judgment is forever banished.

Secondly, salvation means *reconciliation*. By nature, sinful human beings are enemies of God, because God is pure goodness and has a righteous hatred of evil. But when the problem of our sin is dealt with, the way is clear for us to be reconciled to God. We literally become friends of God, rather than enemies. In fact, the Bible goes further and says that we become *children* of God.[32] We're not just friends—we're family.[33]

Thirdly, salvation means *transformation*. As I ex-

---

32. John 1:12; 1 John 3:1.

33. This 'family of God', consisting of the spiritually-adopted brothers and sisters of Christ, is what the New Testament calls 'the church'. Galatians 6:10; Ephesians 2:19; 1 Timothy 3:15; Hebrews 2:11; 1 Peter 2:17; 5:9.

plained earlier, Christianity teaches that we're not merely tainted by sin; we're thoroughly polluted by it. Indeed, we're *enslaved* to sin.[34] We desperately need to be released from captivity to sin—to be 'redeemed', as the Bible puts it. Our corrupt, spiritually diseased hearts need to be healed. In spiritual terms, we're not merely *sick*. No, we're spiritually *dead*—and so we need to be brought back to life.[35] We need a radical supernatural transformation, and that is exactly what those who trust in Christ receive. This is where the third person of the Trinity, the Holy Spirit, plays a key role in our salvation. Since God is the author of life, and the Holy Spirit is a divine person, He has the power to give us the new life we need (what Jesus called 'being born again').[36] Our hearts are supernaturally changed so that instead of being driven by love of sin and self-interest, we're driven by love for God. We aren't immediately made sinless, but we are progressively transformed into less sinful people as the Holy Spirit, by maturing our faith and repentance, conforms us over time to the pattern of self-sacrificial holiness that we see in Jesus Himself.

In sum, the Christian view of salvation means that the problem of sin and its consequences is decisively

---

34. Romans 6:15-23.
35. Ephesians 2:4-5.
36. John 3:1-8.

dealt with. The guilt and penalty of sin are cancelled. The alienation caused by sin is removed. The bondage of sin is broken. The stain of sin is cleansed away.

THE FINAL CHAPTER

Every good story needs a *beginning* and an *ending*, an introduction and a conclusion. Ideally the ending should connect coherently with the beginning, and any problems or crises encountered in the course of the story should be resolved—at least if the story is to have a *happy* ending!

Since worldviews tell stories, a similar principle applies to worldviews. A comprehensive worldview should address not only the *beginning* of history but also its *end*. It should say something about where everything came from and how it all got started, as well as something about where everything is going and how it will all end. The Christian worldview has much to say about both the beginning and the end, and its perspective on the latter is quite stunning.

If Christianity were a play, it would have four acts: Creation, Fall, Redemption and Consummation.[37] We've considered the first three acts already. As Christians view history, we're still in the third act. The Son of God came into our world and secured salvation for all those who

---

37. The word *consummation* means completion or fulfilment.

put their trust in Him. Jesus was born, lived a perfect life, died as a perfect atoning sacrifice for our sins, rose from the dead, and returned to His Father in heaven. The main task He set for His disciples was to *spread the good news of salvation*, so that everyone may hear the message of salvation and have the opportunity to receive it.

But the curtain will eventually fall on this third act. Indeed, it really *has* to come to an end at some point, otherwise God's goodness and power would be in question. After all, despite the salvation that God is working out in our world, this is still a very broken and needy world. It cries out for a final and decisive restoration. We long to see the final victory of God over evil.

The climactic event in the third act—Redemption—is the coming of Jesus Christ into our world: His incarnation, atonement and resurrection. According to the Bible, the climactic event in the fourth act—Consummation—is the *return* of Jesus Christ. Jesus told His disciples that although He had to leave them and return to the Father, He would not only send the Holy Spirit to them but also come a second time once their mission was complete. Just as He physically departed the world, so He will physically return to this world, ushering in a series of events that will bring His redemptive work to complete fulfilment.

In the first place, there will be a *general resurrection*.

Every person who ever lived will be raised to life again, just as Jesus was raised to life again. Immediately following that resurrection there will be a *day of judgment*. All will stand before God, the perfect Judge of the universe, and give an account of what they have done with the lives granted to them.[38] Every good deed will receive its just reward, every sin its just punishment. On the face of it, this is a terrifying prospect, for even the slightest sin is tantamount to cosmic treason and grounds for eternal separation from an absolutely pure and holy God. But those who have been redeemed by Christ will have nothing to fear, because the penalty for their sins has already been paid in full by Him. They will stand before God without guilt—not because of their own goodness, but because of Christ's.[39]

Yet those who did not embrace the gift of salvation will have no such escape. The teaching of the Bible is crystal clear on this point. There are only two possible destinies for each one of us. One destiny is what Jesus called 'eternal life': never-ending fullness of life, utterly free from sin, sadness and suffering. Every pleasure and joy that our Creator originally intended for us will

---

38. Romans 3:6; 14:10. Sometimes the biblical writers say that *Jesus* will be the judge, which underscores the divine authority of Jesus. For example: Acts 10:42; 17:31.

39. Romans 8:1; 8:31-34.

be experienced without hindrance or corruption. Our hearts will overflow with undivided love and adoration! Words are woefully inadequate to describe this glorious prospect; in our current state we can barely begin to grasp what this will be like.[40]

The alternative destiny is a grim and terrifying one, but it is an integral element of the biblical worldview that cannot be sidelined. If there really is an ultimate justice in the universe, there must be a hell as well as a heaven. The alternative to eternal life is eternal death: utter separation from God and thus from the true source of joy and fulfilment. Jesus spoke frequently about hell and used various words to describe it. It is a place of 'fire', 'torment' and 'darkness'. Debates over the degree to which these are metaphors are rather beside the point. What's beyond dispute is that no one in their right mind would want to spend eternity in hell. The prospect is literally beyond our worst nightmares.

The final chapter of the Christian story is the *restoration* of the creation from its fallen and cursed state. In the beginning, God created 'the heavens and the earth'.[41] This original creation was spoiled by sin. In the end, however, God will bring things full circle with a climactic act of *re-creation*. Our broken world will

---

40. 1 Corinthians 2:9.

41. Genesis 1:1.

be refined by a divine fire that purges what is evil and renews what is good, and the outcome will be 'a new heaven and a new earth'.[42] This new creation won't be equal to the original creation—it will far surpass it! The Bible casts the vision of a joyous world in which God's people live in perfect relationship with God and with one another. Their peace and delight will be even greater than that of Adam and Eve before the fall, for they will know and worship God not only as Creator but also as Redeemer. They will dwell forever in a flawless and glorious world with their flawless and glorious Savior, Jesus Christ.

Such is the final chapter of 'the story of the world', according to Christianity. It's a story that's integral to the biblical Christian worldview, and only makes sense in the context of that broader worldview. In this chapter, I've set out the main contours of the Christian worldview in a rather abbreviated fashion: the biblical view of God, the universe, human nature, the basic human problem, God's solution, and so forth. Although I haven't explicitly argued for the *truth* of the Christian worldview yet, I hope you can at least begin to appreciate its consistency and coherence.

But now it's time to directly address the central

---

42. Isaiah 65:17-25; 2 Peter 3:10-13; Revelation 21:1-4.

question of this book: *Why should you believe any of this?* In the remaining chapters I will argue that there are excellent reasons to believe that Christianity is true. In fact, in the final analysis it's the only reasonable option.

4

God is There

In August 2015 several news outlets reported on the case of Gretta Vosper, an ordained minister in the United Church of Canada, who was fighting to keep her job because of certain unorthodox beliefs she had expressed from the pulpit. Not only had Revd Vosper denied that the Bible is the Word of God and that Jesus is the Son of God, she had gone so far as to renounce the existence of God altogether! Apparently this wasn't news to her congregation: she had already proclaimed her atheism in a sermon back in 2001. It's somewhat mysterious why it has taken over a decade for the UCC, the largest Protestant denomination in Canada, to address whether her beliefs (or lack of them) are compatible with her job description.

You don't need to be a Christian to see that there's something quite absurd about the idea of a 'Christian atheist'. A Christian is, after all, a follower of Christ, and one could hardly imagine Jesus telling His disciples, 'Follow me—believing in God is strictly optional!' Christianity without God would be like the Pacific Ocean without water.

Whether God exists—and what *kind* of God exists— is surely one of the most fundamental issues addressed by any worldview. A foundational tenet of the Christian worldview is that God is real; indeed, God is the *ultimate* reality. God is the Absolute Being above and behind all other beings. In this chapter, I want to lay out some excellent reasons for believing that God is real—and not some vague, generic deity, but the God of the Bible, the God that Jesus spoke about. In fact, I will go further and argue that if God isn't real then *nothing* makes any sense in this world.

CAN GOD BE PROVEN?

A great deal of ink has been spilled on the question of whether it's possible to prove that God exists, and if so, what that proof would look like. Skeptics will often insist that while no one can prove that God *doesn't* exist, there's no more evidence for God's existence than for the existence of Santa Claus, the Yeti, the Loch Ness monster and invisible fairies at the end of your garden. What these skeptics often fail to recognize is that the God of the Bible is a fundamentally different kind of being than Santa Claus, the Yeti, and so on, and therefore the way in which one proves God's existence must be fundamentally different too.

Take the Yeti, for example. If the Yeti is real, it's a *physical* being that exists in time and space as part of the physical universe. It could be observed directly with any one of our five senses. (I imagine seeing or hearing the Yeti would be preferable to smelling or tasting it.) Even if the Yeti wasn't *directly* observed, it could well leave indirect physical evidence: giant footprints in the snow, for instance. The way in which we might prove the existence of the Yeti will depend on the *nature* of the Yeti, on what kind of thing it is.

The God of the Bible, however, is not at all like the Yeti. Indeed, according to Christianity God is fundamentally and radically different from every other thing in existence. Unlike the deities of Greek and Roman mythology, God isn't a being who exists *within* the universe, as part of it. Rather, God is a spiritual being who transcends both space and time. God isn't part of the universe, because God *created* the universe. God isn't constrained by space and time, because God *created* space and time. Whereas the universe and everything within it is finite and limited, God is an *infinite* being who is unlimited in all His attributes. God is absolutely perfect in goodness, power, wisdom and knowledge.

One of the unique attributes of God is His absolute independence or self-existence. What this means is that everything other than God depends on God for its existence, but God depends on nothing for His existence. God simply *is*. When Moses asked what name he should use to identify God, the answer he received was deceptively profound: 'I am who I am!'[1] Nothing except God defines God. God is by nature the Absolute Being who defines and sustains every other being.

What all this means is that we can't 'detect' God in the way that we detect things within the universe. God exists at an entirely different level of being than the universe. It's not that God is more ephemeral than other beings like us. Quite the opposite: God is the *most real being of all*, which means we need to steer clear of crude attempts to prove or disprove His existence that treat God as though He were just like any other being.

So how can God's existence be proven? Here's my answer in a nutshell, which I'll unpack in the rest of this chapter. Even though God cannot be directly perceived like the ordinary things within the universe, it turns out that we cannot make sense of the ordinary things we do perceive—and the universe as a whole—*unless* God exists. In short, only a worldview centered on a transcendent,

1. Exodus 3:14.

perfect, personal Creator can make rational sense of the very things we take for granted all the time.

Now that's a very strong claim to make, and I need to do more than just make the claim. I need to give some good reasons to believe it. I will get to those reasons shortly, but before we consider them it's worth taking a moment to reflect on just how much hangs on the question of God's existence.

Whether or not the God of the Bible exists makes all the difference in the world—quite literally! Let's return to the Yeti comparison for a moment. Little of significance hangs on whether the Yeti exists. It would certainly be intriguing to discover that the Yeti is real, and it would keep the media occupied for a week or two, but it would have almost no meaningful impact on our everyday lives. The universe we inhabit would be much the same whether or not the Yeti exists.

Not so with God. If God exists, that affects *everything*, simply because of who God is. If God exists, everything else depends for its existence and nature on God. If God exists, the ultimate reality is *personal* and *rational* and *moral* in nature. If God exists, it follows that the universe has a transcendent personal cause from which it derives its existence, its meaning, its direction, its intelligibility and its moral character. If God exists, life on this planet isn't a cosmic accident. Most important of all, *we* are not a cosmic accident. We were brought into existence by God for a purpose. How could there be anything *more* significant for us than that?

Contrast that worldview—a worldview in which our universe is the creation of a personal God—with the worldview of Naturalism, which is arguably the most prominent alternative in Western society today, at least among intellectuals. Naturalism is the view that *only the natural universe exists*. According to Naturalism, there's nothing 'beyond' or 'behind' the space-time universe, and everything within the universe can be explained scientifically in terms of physics and chemistry. For the Naturalist either the universe came into existence out of nothing with no prior cause or explanation, or the universe has always existed in some form or other.[2]

Naturalism asserts that all of reality—including us— consists at bottom of nothing more than fundamental physical particles and forces, operating according to the laws of physics. Naturalism denies that there are any irreducibly non-physical things, such as spirits or souls. Above all, there is no transcendent Creator. As one

2. One version of the second theory asserts that our universe is just the latest in an eternal series of universes; another proposes that our universe is just one within a 'multiverse' of distinct space-time universes. Despite their differences, these are all variations on the common theme of Naturalism.

influential Naturalist elegantly summarized his creed: 'The Cosmos is all that is or ever was or ever will be.'[3]

The worldview of Naturalism presents a radically different perspective on the universe and our lives. If Naturalism is correct, it follows that reality is *ultimately* non-personal, non-rational and non-moral.[4] The universe we inhabit has no ultimate meaning, purpose, direction or significance. It came from nowhere and it's heading nowhere. The only real laws governing the universe are the laws of physics, which means there's no *moral* order behind anything. The laws of physics are purely descriptive in nature. They tell us how physical things *do* behave, but they have nothing to say about how those things *ought to* behave. The laws of physics are morally blind.

According to Naturalism, then, nothing in the universe is ultimately good or evil. Objectively speaking the universe is simply a clump of physical things doing what physical things do, obeying the laws of physics, and in the final analysis there's nothing more to be said about it. Of course, this worldview has huge implications

---

3. Carl Sagan, *Cosmos* (Random House, 1980), p. 4.

4. By 'non-rational' and 'non-moral' I don't mean *irrational* and *immoral*. (As I'll argue later on, the concepts of irrationality and immorality are ultimately meaningless within a Naturalist worldview.) My point here is only that according to Naturalism the universe isn't governed by a rational mind or a moral purpose.

for how we think about ourselves, because Naturalism implies that the human race, like every other species on our planet, is merely a cosmic accident. No one planned for us to be here. There's no overarching purpose or significance to our lives. The only 'purpose' you can attach to your life is one of your own invention. But in that case your purpose is no more or less valid than mine or anyone else's. If you decide the purpose of your life is to discover a cure for cancer and I decide the purpose of my life is to discover the tastiest doughnut, the universe really doesn't care one way or the other. The same goes for the guy who decides the purpose of his life is to get as much pleasure as he can at other people's expense, even if that causes immense suffering. It's all ultimately arbitrary.

Not all Naturalists have consistently thought through the implications of their worldview, but those who have can be quite forthright about them. Here's how one Naturalist philosopher concisely answers some of the major questions of human existence:

> *Is there a God?* No.
> *What is the nature of reality?* What physics says it is.
> *What is the purpose of the universe?* There is none.
> *What is the meaning of life?* Ditto.
> *Why am I here?* Just dumb luck.
> *Does prayer work?* Of course not.
> *Is there a soul? Is it immortal?* Are you kidding?
> *Is there free will?* Not a chance!

> *What happens to us when we die?* Everything pretty
> much goes on as before, except us.
> *What is the difference between right and wrong, good and
> bad?* There is no moral difference between them.
> *Does history have any meaning or purpose?* It's full of
> sound and fury, but signifies nothing.[5]

Such is the perspective of Naturalism, the most
prominent and intellectually consistent There-Is-No-
God worldview in our day. But to be clear, nothing
I've said so far is intended to *refute* Naturalism. I've
only contrasted two competing worldviews and their
implications so that we can be clear on what's at stake
here and why the existence of God is such a central
and defining issue. With that in mind, let's turn now
to consider some of the reasons why the Christian
worldview makes far more sense than the Naturalist
worldview. I'm going to offer six interrelated arguments
for the existence of God.[6] In each case, I'll identify
something that we take for granted in our lives and
explain why we need God in order to make sense of that
thing.

---

5. Alex Rosenberg, *The Atheist's Guide to Reality: Enjoying Life
   without Illusions* (W. W. Norton & Company, 2011), pp. 2-3.
6. By 'argument' I simply mean a line of reasoning from
   certain beliefs or assumptions (which I presume we share) to
   a conclusion which follows from those beliefs or assumptions.
   I don't mean 'argument' in the sense of a heated disagreement
   or dispute.

GOD AND EXISTENCE

Here's a truth so obvious that it seems almost perverse to mention it: *Something exists*. Even if you doubt everything else, you cannot reasonably doubt that *you* exist. (As the philosopher René Descartes famously argued, you have to exist in order to doubt your own existence!) Most of us happily acknowledge that *many* things exist: stars, mountains, trees, rabbits, buildings, smartphones, and so on. But for those who reflect on such matters, the question arises: *Why?*

Why does anything exist at all?

In a sense, this most obvious of truths—something exists—is a rather surprising one. After all, none of the things in that short list above *had* to exist. Each of them might *not* have existed. The universe could have been very different; it could have existed *without* any of those things. Likewise for anything else in the universe we might care to list. So the existence of all these things begs for an explanation. What accounts for their existence? What accounts for the fact that *anything at all* exists?

Philosophers have a special term for things that exist but didn't have to exist: *contingent*. A contingent thing is one that might *not* have existed, even though it does in fact exist. Its non-existence is logically possible. So, for example, the Eiffel Tower is contingent. It didn't *have* to exist. The French could have decided never to build it in the first place, and it's entirely possible for it to *cease* to exist at some point in the future. The same goes for any man-made object.

Living organisms, however, are also contingent. Take rabbits, for example. Everyone agrees there was a time when no rabbits existed. Rabbits came into existence, of course, but they didn't *have* to. There's nothing impossible about a universe without rabbits (upsetting though the thought might be for rabbit-lovers). The same goes for human beings. You and I are *contingent* beings. Your parents might never have met, in which case you would never have existed. No doubt the world would have been immeasurably poorer for your absence, but that was a real possibility.

The same observation can be extended to any physical or natural object. Take any star you observe in the sky. That star is a contingent thing; it might never have existed. The same is true of each individual atom within that star. *Everything* in the physical universe is contingent. But it's important to see that what is true of the *parts* of the universe is also true of the *whole*. After all, the physical universe isn't a fundamentally different *kind* of thing than its contents. It's just a clump of physical things. The cosmos as a whole is an inconceivably large *physical* thing—and therefore it's a *contingent* thing.[7]

---

7. Some readers may suspect I'm committing the 'fallacy of composition' here. But I'm not arguing from the parts to the whole. I'm simply observing that physical things are by nature contingent, and therefore the physical universe as a whole must be contingent.

With that observation before us, we can move forward with the argument. Any contingent thing needs an explanation for *why* it exists, since it might not have existed. But that explanation can't come from the thing itself. It has to come from *outside* that thing. It makes no sense to say that something brought *itself* into existence, since it would have to exist already in order to do anything at all. So the existence of every contingent thing has to be explained by some *other* thing—and that other thing must be either contingent or non-contingent.

I'm sure you can see where this is heading. If the universe as a whole is contingent, there needs to be an explanation of *why* it exists, and that explanation cannot come from the universe itself or anything within the universe. One of the great difficulties faced by the worldview of Naturalism is that it offers no explanation for the existence of the universe, and thus no explanation for the existence of *anything*, because according to Naturalism only the universe exists. The problem is acute: Naturalism *forbids* any explanation for the existence of the universe, since it insists there's nothing beyond the universe that *could* explain its existence.

In stark contrast, the Christian worldview faces no such difficulty. For that worldview includes three fundamental tenets:

1. God exists.

2. God is *not* a contingent being.

3. God freely chose to use His unlimited power to bring the universe into existence.

Precisely because God is a fundamentally different kind of being than the universe, the puzzle of existence finds a coherent answer. The universe is not self-existent. It has to derive its existence from some other source. But God *by His very nature* is absolutely self-existent. If God had to derive His existence from some other source, He wouldn't be the Absolute Being. He wouldn't be God! (In fact, that other source would be the *real* God.) So the Christian worldview can account for the existence of the universe in a way that the Naturalist worldview simply cannot.

In sum, the obvious truth that *something exists* gives us a compelling reason to believe in God. Existence itself points us to the existence of God.

As it stands, you might think this line of reasoning does nothing to distinguish Christianity from other monotheistic religions. The Christian, however, can ride the argument further down the line. For not only does the universe exist, it exists at multiple levels as a harmony of unity and plurality. At a basic level, the universe contains countless individual physical particles, but they all behave in a unified fashion, obeying the same physical laws. There is both unity (laws) and plurality (particles). At a higher level, the human race is made up of billions of diverse individuals, but we're unified by a common human nature that distinguishes us from other creatures like chimpanzees and manatees.

Since the universe exists as a harmony of unity and plurality, we should expect the *source* of its existence to exhibit a similar harmony of unity and plurality. And that's exactly what the Christian view of God maintains. The Absolute Being is both One and Many: an ultimate unity (one God) and an ultimate plurality (three distinct persons) in perfect harmony.

GOD AND VALUES

One of the things we do all the time, usually without thinking about it, is to make *value* judgments. We'll think or say that something is *good* or *bad*. In extreme cases we'll even use concepts like *perfect* or *evil*. Sometimes these judgments are clearly subjective in the sense that they depend on our own personal tastes or preferences. For example, I'm drinking a cup of coffee as I write this: I think coffee is a *good* thing—I can't get enough of it— but I have friends who don't like coffee at all. Likewise for other things, such as movies: I think Christopher Nolan's *Inception* is a great movie while Steven Spielberg's *Lincoln* is a tedious dud, but I know people who make very different value judgments. (As they say, there's no accounting for taste.)

But not all value judgments are subjective and person-relative in that way. Some are *objective* value judgments, in this sense: when we make those judgments, we're saying that something is good or bad *regardless of anyone's personal tastes or preferences*. For example, the discovery of antibiotics was a *good* thing while the Holocaust was a *bad* thing—indeed, a supremely *evil* thing. No right-thinking person really believes these value judgments are merely matters of personal taste or cultural preference. People may disagree about *which* things are objectively good or bad, but the fact is that everyone makes *some* objective value judgments, whether they recognize it or not.

Now what does this have to do with the existence of God? Here's the argument. Any objective value judgment presupposes some objective *standard* or *criterion* of judgment: some objective standard of *goodness* by which things can be judged. What's more, that standard has to be independent of us, otherwise it wouldn't be truly objective. It can't be reducible to human desires, feelings or preferences—as if the Holocaust was bad for no other reason than that most people didn't like it or want it. (What if most people *had* wanted it?)

Furthermore, that objective standard must represent *pure* goodness. It must be *absolutely* good, otherwise it couldn't serve as the final standard of what is good or bad. If the standard weren't absolutely good—if it were a mixture of good and bad—then there would have to be some *higher* standard by which we judge it to be less than absolutely good. The upshot is that our objective value judgments take for granted that there's some absolute standard or measure of goodness by which everything else can be judged.

So here's the crucial question. Which worldview makes sense of our objective value judgments? Which worldview is most consistent with our assumption that some things are *objectively good* and other things are *objectively bad*? Which worldview affirms that absolute standard of goodness?

As many philosophers have recognized, the Naturalist worldview faces real difficulties in this area. If the universe came from nothing and has no objective meaning or purpose, what sense does it make to say that some things in the universe are objectively good or bad? If everything reduces to physical particles and forces, what basis could there be for objective value judgments? What sense does it make to say that one arrangement of physical particles is any better or worse than any other arrangement of physical particles?

Let me try to put my finger on the basic problem for the Naturalist. If we say that some aspects of the universe are objectively good (e.g. butterflies) and other aspects are objectively bad (e.g. diseases) there must be some standard of goodness *independent* of the universe by which we're judging those different aspects of the universe. And that standard must be *pure* goodness. But according to the Naturalist, *nothing exists except the universe*. It's precisely this problem which has led many Naturalists to deny that our objective value judgments have any meaningful connection with reality.

It should be fairly clear that the Christian worldview doesn't face the same problem. According to the Christian worldview, God is *absolutely good* and God exists independently of the universe. So there is indeed an absolute, ultimate, objective standard of goodness by which things can be judged to be good or bad. In short, something is objectively good if it reflects the character of God, and conforms to the will of God, and something is objectively bad if it's opposed to what is objectively good. So the Christian worldview makes sense of the objective value judgments we make as a matter of routine, including our assumption that such judgments are actually grounded in reality rather than fiction.

The same line of reasoning can be stated in a slightly different way, in terms of our concept of *perfection*. I doubt you believe that the universe is perfect just as it is. I imagine you think the universe could be better than it is right now.

But if we say that the universe is *imperfect*, we're assuming there is some standard or criterion of perfection by which the universe can be judged to be less than perfect. And that standard must be independent of the universe; it must *transcend* the universe, since the universe is subject to it. So what is that standard of perfection? For the Naturalist there's no meaningful answer to that question, which is why Naturalism has to fall back on subjectivism. But for the Christian the answer is obvious: God is the standard of perfection, because the Absolute Being is by definition perfect in every respect. (If we deny that God is perfect, we're tacitly assuming some *other* standard of perfection, some criterion by which we judge God to be less than perfect, in which case that standard is functioning as the real God.)

Once again, something we take for granted in our everyday lives drives us to acknowledge the reality of God. Only on the assumption that God exists can we make sense of the value judgments we make about ourselves, others, and the universe we inhabit.

GOD AND MORALITY

The third argument I want to offer is really an extension of the previous one. I suspect you'll agree that the most important value judgments we make in life are *moral* judgments. We make decisions based on moral values, and we make moral judgments about other people's decisions and actions. We believe that some actions are *good* and *right*, while others are *bad* and *wrong*—in some cases even *wicked* or *evil*. Some of these moral judgments are based on subjective tastes or personal interests, but many times they aren't. They're *objective* moral judgments. When we agree that it's wrong what the Nazis did to the Jews, or what the Islamic State has done to innocent civilians in Iraq and Syria, we don't mean merely that it's wrong *for us* (and by implication, not wrong *for them*). No, we mean that it's morally wrong *period*. It's not just a matter of different personal preferences or cultural traditions. What these murderous people have done is objectively immoral. Indeed, it's *absolutely* immoral.

The moment we say that, however, we're assuming there are moral standards that are objective and absolute. We're presupposing there are moral laws which *transcend* human individuals and human societies. So who or what accounts for these moral standards or laws? Once again, this is a glaring problem for atheistic worldviews like Naturalism. According to such worldviews, the universe has no ultimate meaning or purpose. In the end, there's no right or wrong way for the universe to be. It simply is what it is. The only ultimate laws are the laws of physics. But the laws of physics have nothing to say about *morality*, of course. The laws of physics tell us how things *do* behave, but not how things (including humans) *ought* to behave.

Atheists who want to make objective moral judgments will often try to explain those judgments in terms of cultural conventions (i.e. different societies come to a practical agreement about what behaviors are permissible or impermissible) or human happiness (i.e. morality is basically about what gives people the most pleasure and the least pain). The flaw in such views is that often we make moral judgments which distinguish between different cultures and different pleasures. For example, some cultures have practiced child sacrifice and female genital mutilation, which we judge to be morally wrong—in which case, we're assuming some moral standard that *transcends* human cultures and societies. Likewise, what some people find pleasurable causes distress to others. Some folk get a kick out of other people's unhappiness! So in practice no one treats human pleasures as the final arbiter of good and evil. Rather, we make moral judgments that distinguish between *good* pleasures (e.g. finding happiness in marriage) and *bad* pleasures (e.g. getting aroused by child pornography).

In contrast, the Christian worldview makes sense of our moral judgments. There are transcendent moral laws because there is a transcendent moral *law-giver*. Moral laws cannot come from an impersonal source.

They must come from a personal source, and one with *moral authority*. If the universe is God's creation then God has authority over us. He made us for a purpose and therefore He has the right to say how we should live. Just as the rules of a board game are determined by its inventor, so the rules of human life are determined by our Creator. God's laws have real moral force, but they aren't arbitrary or capricious, because God only commands what is consistent with His perfect love and His good purposes for His creation. In short, God gives us moral laws *for our own good*. They're the Maker's instructions.

Objective moral judgments, then, presuppose the existence of God. But don't just take my word for it. You may be surprised to hear that many atheists *agree* on that point. Friedrich Nietzsche and Jean-Paul Sartre provide two famous illustrations, but I want to focus instead on a more recent example which I find particularly illuminating. Joel Marks is a professor of philosophy at the University of New Haven who for many years wrote a column entitled 'Moral Moments' for the magazine *Philosophy Now*. In 2010 he penned an article entitled 'An Amoral Manifesto', in which he explained why he had become a 'hard atheist', someone who denies both God and morality. His confession is strikingly forthright:

The long and the short of it is that I became convinced that atheism implies amorality; and since I am an atheist, I must therefore embrace amorality … [T]he religious fundamentalists are correct: without God, there is no morality. But they are incorrect, I still believe, about there being a God. Hence, I believe, there is no morality.

Why do I now accept hard atheism? I was struck by salient parallels between religion and morality, especially that both avail themselves of imperatives or commands, which are intended to apply universally. In the case of religion, and most obviously theism, these commands emanate from a Commander; 'and this all people call God,' as Aquinas might have put it. The problem with theism is of course the shaky grounds for believing in God. But the problem with morality, I now maintain, is that it is in even worse shape than religion in this regard; for if there were a God, His issuing commands would make some kind of sense. But if there is no God, as of course atheists assert, then what sense could be made of there being commands of this sort? In sum, while theists take the obvious existence of moral commands to be a kind of proof of the existence of a Commander, i.e. God, I now take the non-existence of a Commander as a kind of proof that there are no Commands, i.e. morality.[8]

Professor Marks is perfectly correct about the connection between God and morality. The only *consistent* atheism

8. Joel Marks, 'An Amoralist Manifesto (Part I)', *Philosophy Now* (August/September 2010).

is 'hard atheism'.[9] Astonishingly, however, he thinks it's more reasonable to disbelieve in God than to believe in morality. Yet what could be more obvious than that killing millions of Jews in gas ovens and slaughtering women and children in the Middle East are really, truly, objectively *morally wrong*? Conscience and consistency conspire together to drive us to God.

GOD AND REASON

Critics of religion often pride themselves on their rationality, and they like to cast the debate in terms of *reason* versus *faith*. Atheists stand on reason, we're told, while religious folk have to fall back on faith. Richard Dawkins, for example, pejoratively refers to religious believers as 'faith-heads' while presiding over the *Richard Dawkins Foundation for Reason and Science*.[10]

In reality, there's no conflict between reason and belief in God, for there are excellent reasons to believe in God. I've discussed some of them already, and there are more to follow. At this point, however, I want to make a more provocative claim: *Our very ability to reason presupposes the existence of God.*

Just as we take for granted our ability to make meaningful moral judgments, so we take for granted our

---

9. 'Soft atheists', according to Professor Marks, are those who reject God but still want to affirm morality.

10. Dawkins set up the foundation on the heels of his bestselling book, *The God Delusion*.

ability to *reason*: to judge between truth and falsehood, to extend our knowledge of the world using logical inferences and evaluation of evidence, and to decide what's reasonable and what's unreasonable. *Everyone* reasons—although clearly some people reason better than others! We take our ability to reason for granted, but it's a truly remarkable thing that we possess the intellectual faculties that we do. Few of us ever reflect deeply on why we have them or how we acquired them. No other species on this planet has the ability to reason as we do. Not only are we able to reason, we're able to recognize and reflect upon our *ability* to reason. We can reason about *reason itself.* (We're doing it right now.)

How then do we account for this truly remarkable human ability, this indispensable feature of our lives? Once again we find that the Christian worldview makes excellent sense of this obvious fact. The ultimate reality is a *rational* reality. God is the supreme intellect. Since God is both perfect and personal, He knows and understands all truths; more than that, God knows and understands *how every truth relates to every other truth*. What this means is that our universe has its source in a rational mind. While there are aspects of it that seem to defy *our* rational understanding, the universe as such isn't intrinsically irrational or unintelligible.

Furthermore, Christianity teaches not only that we were created by God but specifically that we were

116

created *in God's image*. One aspect of that, which we considered earlier, is our capacity to make moral judgments. Another aspect is our capacity to reason. Just as human morality finds its source and explanation in God's absolute goodness, so human rationality finds its source and explanation in God's absolute intelligence.

Despite the pretensions of atheists to have reason on their side, the leading atheistic worldview—Naturalism—faces great difficulties in accounting for our rational faculties. One of those difficulties I'll come to in the next section. But the central problem can be simply stated: Naturalism is committed to the idea that *reason* came from *non-reason*. The physical universe *as such* doesn't have a mind. It doesn't have an intellect or any rational faculties. At the beginning of time, the universe was just a highly compressed lump of matter—and lumps of matter have no thoughts at all, never mind *rational* thoughts. So the Naturalist has to believe that rational beings arose out of entirely non-rational materials and processes. That's no easier to swallow than the idea that moral beings arose out of entirely non-moral materials and processes.

The most common explanation offered by Naturalists is an evolutionary one: we humans gradually developed the ability to reason over millions of years by a process of natural selection. Our reason gives us a clear survival advantage, so it is argued. This explanation faces several formidable objections, one of which I'll develop in the next section: only *conscious* beings can reason, but there's no good evolutionary explanation for how physical processes alone could produce conscious minds.

But there's another strike against the Naturalist's evolutionary account. Most of the organisms on this planet survive and reproduce perfectly well—far more efficiently than humans!—without the slightest ability to reason. If evolution is driven by natural selection, as Darwin's theory dictates, then evolution doesn't care a whit for what an organism *believes*. It only cares about how an organism *behaves*. From an evolutionary perspective, it doesn't matter whether an organism has true beliefs, false beliefs, or no beliefs at all, as long as the organism can effectively preserve and pass on its genes. Evolution isn't *truth*-directed. It's only *survival*-directed.

But our faculty of reason *is* truth-directed. The very purpose of reason is to guide us towards truth. What's more, humans possess many higher intellectual powers, such as the capacity to understand advanced calculus, music theory, poetry and philosophy, none of which confer any obvious advantage when it comes to biological survival and reproduction, the driving forces of evolution. (It's tempting to suggest that people with highly advanced intellects are at a *disadvantage* in those areas.)

In fact, when we take into account what most humans actually believe, the Naturalist faces something of a conundrum. Either evolution is truth-directed or it isn't. If evolution isn't truth-directed, then the Naturalist has no basis for assuming that his intellectual faculties can be trusted to guide him towards truth, in which case he ought to doubt the truth of his own beliefs—including his belief in Naturalism! But if evolution is (somehow) truth-directed, we have to wonder why most people today are religious. Why has evolution tended to favor beliefs which, according to Naturalists, are so radically out of step with reality?[11]

In the end, the crucial question is this: Which worldview gives us the most reasonable account of reason itself? One in which our reason has its source in a Higher Reason or one in which our reason has its source in no reason at all? If our very ability to reason depends on God, nothing could be more contrary to reason than denying God.

GOD AND MIND

Pause for a moment and reflect on what you're doing right now. You're looking at a page in a book. You're reading words, strung together into sentences, and you're

---

11. Naturalists will commonly reply that religion evolved as a survival mechanism. But that response only reinforces my point: evolution is survival-directed, not truth-directed.

interpreting those sentences to grasp their meanings. Some of those sentences make assertions, and you're subconsciously evaluating those assertions, considering whether they're true or false.

While those internal mental processes are going on, you're also experiencing various sensory impressions from your immediate environment. You can see the shapes of the letters on the page. You're conscious of the contrast between the text and the background. You can also feel the weight and texture of the book as you hold it in your hand and run your fingers over its surfaces. If you shift your attention, you'll become aware of distinct sounds around you, such as people talking nearby, background music, or traffic in the distance. Perhaps the taste of your last meal or cup of coffee lingers in your mouth. I could go on, but you get the point: at each moment you're subject to a vivid, multifaceted, conscious experience of the world, not to mention thousands of complex internal thought processes.

All of this is possible only because you possess a *conscious mind* distinct from your physical body. Indeed, you're not merely a conscious being—you're a *self-conscious* being. You're conscious of your own consciousness. You're able to reflect on your own conscious experiences. You're able to think about your own thought processes.

What does any of this have to do with God? The argument I want to develop in this section was hinted at in the previous section, where I argued that reason itself is reason to believe in God. There is, of course, a close connection between *mind* and *reason*. A mind is a prerequisite for reason. Only beings with minds have the ability to reason, because reasoning necessarily involves beliefs and ideas. Reasoning requires *thoughts*, and thoughts exist only in minds. Furthermore, minds exhibit *consciousness*, which offers a distinctive first-person perspective on the world. Each of us has a conscious perspective on the world that's unique and distinct from everyone else's. As beings with minds as well as bodies, we're able to have experiences of the world and to revise our beliefs and ideas accordingly.[12]

The fact that we have conscious minds is another thing we take for granted. It's so obvious and familiar

---

12. One common comeback is that computers are able to reason even though they don't have conscious minds. Strictly speaking, however, computers only *simulate* reason. They don't literally reason in the way that we do, because they don't literally have thoughts, beliefs, or ideas. Computers have no awareness or understanding of what they do. They have no concepts of truth, logic, or reason. What's more, the 'reasoning' that computers do (which is really nothing more than manipulating symbols based on preprogrammed rules and instructions) is entirely dependent on prior human reasoning. A computer is just a sophisticated tool for assisting humans in their reasoning—an extension of an abacus or a slide-rule.

to us that we don't recognize just how remarkable it is. As we evaluate competing worldviews, it's worth asking this question: *How did we come to possess the minds that we do?* Indeed, how is it that there are *any* conscious minds within this physical universe?

One of the oldest philosophical questions concerns how *mind* is related to *matter*, the physical stuff of rocks and trees and human bodies. After all, minds are so very different in nature from material objects. So did mind precede matter? Or did matter precede mind, such that mind is a product of matter?

Worldviews offer different takes on these questions. According to the worldview of Naturalism, *matter preceded mind*. In the beginning the universe was pure matter, but over the course of billions of years, through gradual, undirected evolutionary processes, physical organisms developed conscious minds. On this view, mind is a product of matter—more precisely, an accidental *by-product* of blind material forces.

Some hardcore Naturalists have gone even further in their commitment to materialism by denying that there really are such things as minds distinct from matter. You have to wonder what's going through their minds! (As the philosopher John Searle once quipped: If you doubt that you really have a conscious mind, just give yourself a hard pinch.)

The difficulty for Naturalism is that it's very hard to conceive how minds could arise out of purely material processes. Conscious minds have very distinctive features, such as a first-person subjective perspective on the world and a capacity for thoughts, feelings and experiences. Such features are so thoroughly different from physical properties such as mass, energy and size, that there seems to be a fundamental discontinuity between the mental and the physical. No scientist or philosopher has come anywhere close to explaining how conscious minds could be generated by non-conscious physical structures, no matter how complex those structures become. Increasing the complexity of something doesn't result in a fundamentally different *kind* of thing coming into existence: a self-conscious subject of thoughts and experiences. A highly complex physical structure is still nothing more than a physical structure.

Naturalists will often appeal to evolution to explain our advanced mental capacities. They'll argue that possessing a conscious mind gives an organism an evolutionary advantage, and a more sophisticated mind offers an even greater advantage, thus evolution can explain (at least in broad terms) how our remarkable minds came into existence. This sounds plausible until you recognize the basic flaw in this argument: *Naturalistic evolution cannot explain how consciousness appeared in the first place.* Evolutionary forces can only operate on things that *already* exist. Natural selection can only favor a conscious organism over a non-conscious one if a conscious organism is there to be favored.

Naturalists also point to the fact that human mental activity is closely correlated with physical brain processes as evidence that our minds are the product of purely material causes. Neuroimaging technologies, for example, reveal that certain kinds of thoughts and experiences correspond with neurons firing in particular areas of the brain. However, as statisticians often have to remind us, correlation doesn't imply causation— and even if it did, it wouldn't tell us the *direction* of the causation.[13] Observing that two very different things are closely integrated doesn't show that one is the product of the other, but it does invite us to consider how and why they came together in the first place.

Worldviews which imply that rational, conscious minds developed late in the history of the universe, as the chance outcome of purely material processes, face

---

13. In fact, we take it for granted that there's causation in both directions between the mind and the body. If you stick a pin in your thumb and experience pain as a result, that's body-to-mind causation. If you think of a number and then say it out loud, that's mind-to-body causation. One of the great problems faced by Naturalism is explaining how there can be genuine mind-to-body causation if the universe is at bottom just a closed system of material causes.

some serious philosophical challenges.[14] The Christian worldview isn't one of them, however, since it affirms that *mind preceded matter*. Not human minds, of course, but *God's* mind. God is an eternal, self-existent, transcendent, personal being with a *mind*—and not just any mind, but a perfect, absolute, infinite mind. Furthermore, God created a universe that had both material and mental aspects from the outset: He created humans with minds as well as bodies. Not only can we physically manipulate the universe with our bodies, we can *think about* the universe with our minds. Our finite minds aren't the first minds to exist in the universe; on the contrary, our human minds are dependent on—one might even say modeled on—an eternal divine mind. We are literally designed to think God's thoughts after Him.

This view of the universe and our place in it has some profoundly important implications. Here's one of them: because the material and mental aspects of the universe both have their source in God, we can have confidence that our minds are 'fitted' to understand the physical universe, which is one of the most basic assumptions of science.

And that leads me to my sixth argument.

---

14. For a more detailed discussion of these challenges, see Stewart Goetz and Charles Taliaferro, *Naturalism* (Eerdmans, 2008); J. P. Moreland, *The Recalcitrant Imago Dei: Human Persons and the Failure of Naturalism* (SCM Press, 2009).

GOD AND SCIENCE

Science is an indisputably wonderful thing. All of us benefit daily in thousands of ways from the advancements of science, whether we recognize it or not. I'm currently writing this book on a pretty sophisticated laptop computer, the product of decades of scientific research. I'm sitting in a café equipped with electric lights, wireless internet and air conditioning (thankfully, because it's nearly 100°F outside). From my armchair I can see the car in which I drove to the café. In the distance, an airplane is descending for landing. I can scarcely imagine the many scientific inventions that were used to grow and harvest the coffee beans, to transport them to this location, and to create the near-perfect cup of French Roast that I'm sipping. And that's just a small selection of examples of how science has changed our lives for the better. (Of course, we should also recognize that science has also been used for many *evil* purposes, which points us back to the earlier arguments from value and morals.)

Atheists who claim to have reason on their side will often insist they have science on their side too. They'll cite statistics about how scientists are less likely to believe in God than non-scientists. They'll argue that science has disproven many of the central claims of Christianity: for example, that the theory of evolution has discredited the biblical account of human origins. It's important for

Christians to address such challenges, but I want to do something else here: to dig below the surface of these objections into the foundations of science itself. I'm going to argue that science is only possible *because God exists*. In other words, the very existence and success of science depend on God.

It's rarely recognized that science rests on a whole host of philosophical assumptions about the universe and about human beings that science itself cannot justify. No scientific experiment can prove these assumptions; rather, scientists have to take them for granted. But if those assumptions were false, science itself would be futile. It would take a whole other book to explore all of the presuppositions of science, so I will only mention a selection here.

In the first place, scientific work takes for granted the existence of *objective moral values*. For example, scientists have a moral duty to be thorough and careful in their research, and to be honest and accurate when they publish their results. Indeed, the whole scientific enterprise is driven by a value judgment, namely, that it's *good* to understand how the natural world operates, and that we *ought* to pursue and promote truth and knowledge in the natural sciences. Furthermore, we take for granted that science should be used for *objectively good purposes*, rather than to advance personal agendas, partisan political ideologies, and so on. But as I argued earlier, atheism doesn't comport at all well with the idea of objective value judgments.

Leaving aside the moral dimension of scientific work, however, there are other underlying assumptions of science that expose our dependence on God. Science can only be pursued by beings with higher intellects and conscious minds, with the ability to make reliable observations of the physical world and rational inferences based on those observations. Indeed, science is founded on the assumption that our sensory faculties are equipped to give us accurate empirical information about the universe we inhabit. Scientists take for granted that how the world *appears to us* is a generally reliable picture of how the world *actually is*. That's not something science itself can prove, precisely because science has to presuppose it. It would be circular reasoning to use our sensory faculties to prove the reliability and accuracy of our sensory faculties. So on what rational basis do scientists make this crucial assumption?

Scientific investigation rests on two further assumptions: first, that the universe is an orderly and rational place, and second, that the orderliness and rationality of the universe aligns with the orderliness and rationality of our minds. The idea that our minds are equipped to discover and understand the basic laws of the universe rests on both of these assumptions. Think about it for a moment. The universe didn't *have* to be an orderly and rational place. There's nothing logically contradictory about the idea of a universe that is chaotic and unpredictable, without rhyme or reason. When we formulate theories about the laws of nature, such as the laws of gravity, we assume those laws apply in the same way across space and time. We assume those laws will be the same in the future as they have been in the past. We assume those laws operate in other galaxies in the same way they operate in our own galaxy. In short, we assume that nature is basically *orderly* and *uniform*, such that we can discover general laws of nature and exploit them for technological purposes.

But once again, science itself cannot *prove* that nature is basically orderly and uniform. It's impossible for humans to directly observe the universe at every point in space and time. Only God could know in advance that the universe is basically orderly and rational. God would know that, of course, because God would be *responsible* for it. God arranged it that way!

I trust you can see, then, that science rests on a host of philosophical assumptions, none of which science itself can prove. Science can be no more rational than the foundations on which it stands. Yet it's extremely difficult to rationally justify those foundational assumptions from an atheistic perspective. If the universe is a gigantic metaphysical accident, with no rational mind directing and governing it—as atheists must believe—why on earth should we assume that it operates in an orderly and rational fashion? And why should we assume that our minds are equipped to accurately perceive and understand it?[15]

In contrast to atheistic worldviews such as Naturalism, the Christian worldview provides a firm foundation for science. If the universe is the creation of a personal God, whose mind is supremely rational and orderly, and if our minds are designed and equipped by God to discover truths about the natural world, then it makes perfect sense to pursue science—and we have an explanation for why science has been so *successful*. Moreover, the Christian worldview also provides the moral framework within which science can flourish and promote the common

---

15. I haven't even touched on other issues such as the importance of *mathematics* for science. One of the guiding principles of science is that the universe reflects a mathematical orderliness and can be described in mathematical terms. As many scientists and philosophers have noted, however, the intimate connection between objects in the universe (which are visible and physical in nature) and numbers (which are neither visible nor physical in nature) is quite remarkable and begs for some explanation. For atheists, there is no obvious reason for the deep connection between physics and mathematics; it's just an inexplicable brute fact—and a very fortunate one! For Christians, on the other hand, it's not at all surprising that the universe would reflect a deep mathematical order, since it's the creation of a Master Mathematician.

good. It's no surprise, then, that the pioneers of modern science such as Johannes Kepler, Robert Boyle, Isaac Newton and Michael Faraday were believers in God who looked at the natural world through the lens of a basically biblical worldview.[16] The oft-repeated charge that Christianity is anti-science couldn't be more mistaken. When we think more deeply about the kind of worldview on which science rests, we can see that the very opposite is true. *Science itself depends on God.*

That being the case, we should expect that over time the discoveries of science will support belief in God. I believe that's exactly what we find, although we do need to recognize some qualifications:

- Scientists—like everyone else—are fallible human beings, and their theories are always subject to revision in light of new observations and insights.

- Scientists—like everyone else—have world-views which shape how they interpret evidence and which scientific theories they find most attractive and plausible.

- We need to distinguish between *supposed* discoveries of science (some of which have now been discredited) and *genuine* discoveries of science.

- Scientists disagree among themselves as to exactly what the scientific method has discovered.

---

16. Nancy R. Pearcey and Charles B. Thaxton, *The Soul of Science: Christian Faith and Natural Philosophy* (Crossway, 1994).

Such caveats aside, however, I would contend that the more we learn about the natural universe—and especially our small corner of it—the more evidence we find for a biblical worldview. For example, we've learned from the laws of thermodynamics that the universe hasn't always existed. If the past were infinite, the universe would have completely 'run down' by now. The universe must have had a first moment of existence. So either it simply popped into existence for no reason, with no explanation, or it was brought into existence by some transcendent cause.

We've also learned that the universe as a whole, and our own solar system in particular, appear to be 'fine-tuned' in numerous ways to support the existence of organic life. If the laws of nature had been even slightly different than they are, no habitable planets or solar systems would ever have formed. In fact, the evidence indicates that our own solar system is fine-tuned not merely to support organic life, but to accommodate *conscious* organisms and to promote *scientific investigation* by those conscious organisms.[17] The odds of all this happening by sheer luck are so miniscule as to rule out chance as a serious explanation. As more than one scientist has noted, it appears that the cosmos has been rigged. (Sir Fred Hoyle, the eminent astronomer and

---

17. Guillermo Gonzales and Jay W. Richards, *The Privileged Planet* (Regnery Publishing, 2004).

life-long atheist, is said to have complained that the universe looks like 'a put-up job'.)

Discoveries in chemistry and biology are pointing in the same direction as physics and astronomy. Ongoing research into the origins of life has only underscored how incredibly unlikely it is that the first living cells arose by a combination of natural chemical processes and chance events; on the contrary, the basic building-blocks of organic life bear the distinguishing marks of design. The origin of DNA is particularly perplexing for atheists, because DNA carries complex coded information analogous to computer software. Information can only be generated by intelligent sources, not by mindless natural processes. How do you get software without a programmer?[18]

The scientific challenges to Naturalism don't stop there. Atheists rely on the Darwinian theory of evolution to explain the diversity and complexity of living organisms, and they'll invariably point to progressions in the fossil record as Exhibit A. On closer examination, however, the evidence from palaeontology is more consistent with the activity of an Intelligent Designer than with undirected naturalistic evolution. The fossil record exhibits 'leaps' of complexity and diversity that

---

18. Stephen C. Meyer, *The Signature in the Cell* (HarperOne, 2010).

simply don't fit with the Darwinian theory of evolution, which posits the gradual, step-by-step emergence of new species.[19] The same goes for the astonishingly complex biochemical systems within the living cells that make up our bodies. The more scientists uncover about the details of these microscopic biological factories, the more intractable becomes the problem of explaining how they could have originated by blind natural processes alone.[20] Other examples could be added, such as recent research into the natural limits of evolution, but the point has been made. As scientific understanding has grown, the credibility of atheism has withered.

To be clear, I'm not trying to make a scientific case for Christianity here. I have a more modest goal: to point out that when it comes to scientific arguments, there are always two sides to the debate, and we ought to give a fair hearing to both sides. No less importantly, we must appreciate the crucial role that worldviews play in the way we approach science. Our worldviews inevitably influence how we interpret evidences and evaluate theories. It's naïve to think that any worldview can be proven or disproven by science alone.

Atheists have promoted a narrative of conflict between science and belief in God, but the conflict is more imagined

19. Stephen C. Meyer, *Darwin's Dilemma* (HarperOne, 2014).
20. Michael J. Behe, *Darwin's Black Box*, 2nd ed. (Free Press, 2006).

than real. Indeed, at the deepest level—the worldview level—the opposite is true: the real conflict lies between science and *disbelief* in God. Atheistic worldviews can't account for why science is reasonable and successful, because they can't provide any rational justification for the foundational assumptions of science. Ironically, then, atheistic scientists have to live by faith! Or to put the point more provocatively: they're tacitly depending on a radically different worldview—a God-centered worldview—whenever they engage in their scientific work.

Does God Really Need To Be Proven?

I hope by now I've been able to persuade you that there are excellent reasons to believe in a transcendent personal God who created and sustains the universe. I've argued that we need to acknowledge the reality of God in order to make sense of various things we take for granted and depend on every day: existence, values, morality, reason, mind and science. But it's worth asking whether any of the arguments I've given are actually *necessary*. Do we really need arguments like these as a basis for belief in God?

Actually, no. Indeed, from a Christian perspective that would be quite a bad thing because it takes some serious intellectual effort and aptitude to understand such arguments. Christianity isn't just for intellectuals.

It's for everyone. You don't need to be a black belt in philosophical ju-jitsu to know that God is real. On the contrary, the Bible teaches that the existence of a personal creator is *plainly evident to everyone* from His creation. God's fingerprints are everywhere! Every single element of the universe, from the magnificent spiraling galaxies to the tiniest snowflake, offers evidence of its divine authorship.

When we survey a beautiful landscape or gaze at a glorious sunset; when we delight at the delicate beauty of a butterfly's wings; when we marvel and rejoice at a newborn baby; when we feel the prick of the moral law within us; when we have a deep sense that our lives are not merely a great cosmic accident; when we experience all of these things, and many others beside, it's literally the most natural thing in the world to believe that there is a Creator behind them. It actually takes some concerted mental effort to *suppress* belief in God![21] Knowing that there is a God is as natural and normal as knowing that there is a distinction between right and wrong and that our lives actually *count* for something.

So if the Creator's existence is so evident, why are there atheists? And why do religious people have

---

21. A revealing remark by the atheistic scientist Francis Crick nicely illustrates the point: 'Biologists must constantly keep in mind that what they see was not designed, but rather evolved.' Francis Crick, *What Mad Pursuit* (Basic Books, 1988), p. 138.

disagreements about God? Again, Christianity has its answer: although everyone knows some basic truths about God through His creation, we suppress this knowledge because we don't *like* those truths. Admittedly that sounds perverse on the face of it. Why would anyone *not* want to know the truth about God? The problem is not that we don't want the truth, but rather that we don't want *that* truth. We want the truth to be something else! The Christian view is that in our natural fallen state our ambitions and desires are corrupted, so that we're profoundly self-centered rather than God-centered. The thought of a God who has absolute authority over our lives, who makes moral demands and to whom we're morally accountable, makes us extremely uncomfortable. And we have a remarkable capacity to rationalize away things that make us uncomfortable.

Therefore, from a Christian perspective, if someone has trouble believing in God then the problem is internal rather than external. Unbelief isn't due to a shortage of available evidence or reasons. It's not that belief in God doesn't make sense. On the contrary, *only* belief in God makes sense in the end. When atheists and agnostics live as though the universe is a rational, orderly place, as though there are objective moral standards, as though their fellow humans have real dignity and worth, and as though their own lives have genuine significance, they betray their debt to a biblical worldview and unwittingly confirm their dependence on God.

So those who claim to be 'honest skeptics' need to apply an honest skepticism to their own hearts. As the Bible warns, 'The heart is deceitful above all things'.[22] Indeed, the human capacity for self-deception knows no bounds. We can even deceive ourselves about whether we're self-deceived! We can be truly perverse: disbelieving things because we don't *want* them to be true, and then working hard to find some kind of rational justification for our doubts, all the while patting ourselves on the backs for being 'rational freethinkers' who 'just follow the evidence'. The grand irony is this: if it weren't for God, there would be no rational thinkers at all and no universe to be rationally understood.

One of the central tenets of the Christian worldview is that *God is there*. I've explained why we should believe that to be true. But Christianity is much more than belief in God. It proclaims that God has revealed Himself not only in the orderliness of the natural universe and in the human conscience, but also in a unique *book*— the Bible—and in a unique *person*—Jesus Christ. Why should anyone believe those other things? That's the question we'll consider in the next two chapters.

---

22. Jeremiah 17:9.

5

God is Not Silent

Christians believe not only that God is real, but that God has spoken to us in the Bible. That's why Christians refer to the Bible as 'God's Word', even though it has human authors. The Bible itself claims that those human authors were inspired and directed by a Divine Author, such that God Himself is the ultimate author of the Bible. If that's the case, then what the Bible says, *God* says.

No doubt to many skeptics this seems quite incredible and bizarre. Why do Christians believe this? Do Christians have philosophical or scientific *proofs* that the Bible is God's Word? I'll argue in this chapter that there are solid grounds for believing that God has spoken in the Bible, but I want to concede at the outset that the arguments I'll develop here aren't the *primary* basis for Christian convictions about the Bible. So what is?

HEARING GOD'S VOICE

Let me set things up with an analogy. Imagine that your phone rings, but you don't have caller ID activated so you don't know the identity of the caller before you pick up. You answer the phone, and the person on the other end says, 'Hey, it's me!'

The chances are you've received a call just like that. When you consider it from a strictly logical perspective, the caller's statement couldn't fail to be true. ('Why, of course it's *you*! Who else could it be?') Theoretically, *anyone* could make that statement—even a complete stranger. The words spoken don't contain any specific information about the identity of the caller.

Or do they? I'd wager that when a person calls you and says, 'It's me', 99 per cent of the time you'd know immediately who it is. One reason is that only certain people would identify themselves to you in that way. Another reason is that *you would immediately recognize their voice*. When I get an 'It's me!' call, the person speaking is usually my wife, and sometimes she doesn't even begin with 'It's me'—she just starts telling me what she needs to tell me, and I know it's her right away!

It's not as though I go through some process of *reasoning* to figure out who it is. I don't deduce her identity from the features of her voice and the circumstances of the phone call:

> Hmm ... This is the voice of a woman ... around 40 years old ... with a Scottish accent ... she apparently knows me well ... I therefore deduce that it's probably my wife!

Rather, I know immediately and intuitively that it's my wife speaking to me. I directly perceive it's my wife. So here's the point of the analogy. In a similar fashion, Christians don't typically *deduce* that God is the ultimate author of the Bible via some elaborate process of reasoning. Instead, they *directly perceive* that God is speaking to them through the Bible. They read the Bible, or they hear it read to them, and they *recognize* the voice of God. The experience is difficult to capture in words, but the basic conviction is this: 'There's something very special about this book. This isn't a merely human book. This is *God* speaking to me.'

But here's the thing: none of this comes *naturally*. The ability to recognize the voice of God speaking in the Bible is a *supernatural* one. This is what Christian theologians have called 'the internal witness of the Holy Spirit'. Just as the Holy Spirit supernaturally inspired the *writers* of the Bible, so He also supernaturally illuminates the *readers* of the Bible. The first time this happens to a person it's as though 'the lights go on' and they see the Bible for what it really is. Or to shift the metaphor to another sense-organ: God gives them ears to hear His voice speaking to them in the Bible.

I want to be quite clear here. None of the above is meant to be an *argument* for the Bible. If you don't already believe the Bible is divinely inspired, none of the above will give you any reason to think otherwise. At this point I'm only explaining *what the Christian perspective is*. I'm not offering you reasons to believe it—not yet, anyway. But there is a take-home point for non-believers: if you're serious about wanting to know whether Christian claims about the Bible are true, *the best thing to do is simply to read the Bible for yourself.*

The sad reality is that most people who reject Christianity have never actually taken the time to read the Bible for themselves. What's more, many of those who do so approach the Bible with the express intention of *not* believing it. If someone reads the Bible having pretty much decided in advance that it couldn't be from God, it's hardly surprising when they come away unmoved by it. Why would God approve that kind of prejudicial attitude? The proper attitude to encountering the Bible shouldn't be one of incredulity—but neither should it be one of credulity. Rather, the Bible should be approached with an attitude of sincerity, humility and openness to hearing God speak.

So if you're serious about investigating Christianity but you haven't yet read the Bible—or at least significant parts of it—then if nothing else you owe it to yourself to read it with an open mind and an expectant attitude.

I would recommend, however, that you don't read it from the first page to the last, in the order it's usually arranged. That's because the Bible is really a collection of books—a library of books—rather than one single book. If you wanted to read all the books in a library, I imagine you wouldn't simply read them in the order they're arranged on the shelves. You'd pick out the books that are most immediately accessible and readable.

With that principle in mind, I'd recommend that you read the four Gospels first—Matthew, Mark, Luke and John—which give four complementary accounts of the life and teachings of Jesus. After that, perhaps read the book of Acts, which records some of the remarkable events that followed the crucifixion of Jesus. Next read some of the letters written by the apostle Paul, one of the earliest and most influential converts to Christianity. Start with his letters to the Romans and to the Ephesians, which explain in detail what it means to be 'saved' by Jesus. Sooner or later you'll need to dive into the Old Testament, beginning with the books of Genesis and Exodus, which lay the foundations for the biblical worldview: who God is, where we came from, what's wrong with the world, and how God plans to make things right again.

So if you haven't read the Bible, let me encourage you to make that your next reading project. You have little to lose—and possibly everything to gain.

HAS GOD SPOKEN?

As I noted above, most Christians don't come to believe that the Bible is God's Word through sophisticated philosophical, scientific, or historical arguments. Instead, they come to perceive it immediately through a direct supernatural illumination. And there's nothing particularly odd or outlandish about that. If God can give us ordinary sensory faculties that allow us to perceive things in the natural world, then He also has the power to give people direct insight into spiritual matters, specifically, to perceive His own voice speaking to them in the Bible. But that doesn't mean there's no place for objective arguments or evidence when it comes to the Bible. Quite the contrary: I think there are excellent reasons to believe that God has spoken in the Bible, and I want to turn now to explore those reasons.

Here's a preview of my argument. I suggested in chapter 2 that one of the tests for evaluating worldviews is the test of *coherence*. The more coherent a worldview is—the better it fits together internally—the more reason we have to believe it. I'm going to make the case that a God-Speaks worldview is more coherent than a God-Doesn't-Speak worldview. Furthermore, when we consider the alternatives, the Christian worldview is the only credible candidate among the God-Speaks worldviews out there.

In the previous chapter I argued that only a worldview centered on a transcendent, absolute, personal, creator God can make sense of the things we take for granted. But why should we think this God would *speak* to us? Christianity emphasizes that God is *personal*, as opposed to some kind of impersonal cosmic force or power. Christianity also teaches that God created humans 'in His own image'—that is to say, we humans are also *personal* beings who reflect God's personal attributes at a finite level. We're able to think, reason, exercise imagination, make plans and choices, show affections, and enter into loving relationships with others. This implies that God intended us to have a *personal* relationship with him, as well as with one another. The idea that a personal God would create other personal beings but *not* relate to them in a personal way isn't coherent. It doesn't make sense on the face of it. This becomes especially clear when we recognize that God is perfect in goodness and love, and thus God wants the *best* for His creatures. In our case, the highest good we could experience would be an intimate personal relationship with our Creator. No matter how good our relationships with other humans might be, they cannot begin to compare to a relationship with God!

But how would God enter into a personal relationship with us? What would characterize that relationship?

When we reflect on the personal relationships we form with other human beings, it's clear that *language* is an essential component of those relationships. Verbal communication is the normal means by which we initiate and develop personal relationships. I doubt you can think of any relationship you have with another person that *doesn't* depend on language. Our capacity for verbal communication—to express our thoughts and our feelings in language—is another unique feature of humans that distinguishes us from other creatures. We're able to *speak*. Speech is the primary means by which we relate to one another.[1]

Now let's move the argument along another step or two. If God is personal and unlimited in power, then surely God is *also* able to speak, even if the manner in which God speaks differs from ours. How could God create us with the power to verbally communicate and yet lack that power Himself? Again, the very idea is incoherent. But now we're in a position to put these observations together. If a personal God is going to enter into personal relationships with His personal creatures, and the normal means of initiating and sustaining personal relationships is through language, then *we*

---

1. What about sign language? Well, sign language is still *language*! It's essentially visible speech as an alternative to audible speech. It's another form of verbal communication.

should expect God to speak to us. Once we connect the dots between the kind of God who must exist, the kind of beings we are, and the kind of relationship we would have with God, we can see that the idea of a *silent* God is lacking in coherence.

An analogy may help to reinforce this point. Imagine for a moment that you're a young person with the good fortune to have parents who are loving, wise, resourceful and wealthy. They're just the kind of parents whose sage counsel would be invaluable as you try to navigate the complexities and challenges of modern life. But they also happen to live on another continent. Nevertheless, they've gone to the trouble and expense of installing a special video-phone system in your home, with a direct connection to their own home, which allows them to call and talk with you at any time. Everything is in place for your parents to communicate with you.

Now add the following detail to the scenario. Despite the fact that the means of communication with your parents is available, *they never actually call you*. Not once. The video-phone just sits there, silent and redundant. And when you try to call them, no one answers! Wouldn't that be extraordinarily odd? Surely the overwhelming expectation is that your parents *would* communicate with you. The scenario in which they have the means to speak to you, and yet they don't actually do so, isn't a coherent one. It doesn't make sense. For much the same reason, any worldview which says that God *exists*, but denies that God *speaks*, doesn't make sense on the face of it.

It's often thought that the presence of evil and suffering in the world gives us reason not to believe in God. I'd argue that the very opposite is true, at least if we're talking about the God of the Bible. In the first place, the very concept of evil presupposes an ultimate, objective standard of goodness; without such a standard, any distinction between good and evil will be arbitrary or subjective. As I argued in the previous chapter, only a personal absolute God can supply that ultimate, objective standard of goodness. What's more, the presence of evil and suffering actually *heightens* the expectation that God will speak to us. Our world is a mess, largely because we have made a mess of it. We desperately need to hear our Creator's voice: to hear divine words of wisdom, guidance, comfort and hope. Would a God of perfect love and compassion remain utterly silent in the face of our predicament?

How Has God Spoken?

If it's reasonable to believe that God is there, it's also reasonable to believe that God has spoken. The next question to ask is: *How has God spoken?*

How should we expect God to speak to us? We need to beware of unwarranted speculation here. We mustn't

148

jump to conclusions about how God would or should speak to us. That's His prerogative, not ours. God might well speak to us in a variety of ways and means. Nevertheless, there's good reason to think that if God were to speak to us, He would do so in a *publicly accessible* way. After all, the most important things God would have to say to us would be applicable to human beings *in general*, not just individuals or subgroups. But in that case God's words would have to be generally available to human beings, at least in principle.

By way of comparison, think of the President or Prime Minister of a nation who needs to convey an important message to all the citizens of that nation. In theory he or she could communicate that message to each citizen privately and individually. It makes far more sense, however, for the leader to communicate that message in a public and objectively verifiable way. For then not only does everyone receive the message, but everyone knows that everyone else received the same message as well. It's a *shared* communication.

It's certainly possible for God to speak to humans privately and individually. Christianity doesn't deny that, and the Bible indicates that it occasionally happens (although, significantly, the Bible still fills us in on what God said on those occasions). But if God were to speak *only* privately and individually, there would be no public, objective way to resolve disagreements about what God *has* said. It would always be one person's word against another. Suppose I came to you and said that God has spoken to me—in the privacy of my own home—and told me that I need to relieve you of your 60-inch HDTV, the contents of your wine rack, and your BMW convertible. (Trust me: God told me it's for your own good!) I suspect you'd take issue with my claims. But how could you argue against them if there's no publicly accessible expression of God's will or God's commands? On the other hand, if there's a divine revelation which is objectively knowable and publicly available—something that *anyone* in principle could point to as God's Word—then there's a meaningful basis for settling such disagreements.

For closely related reasons, it also makes sense to assume that God would arrange for His communication to be *written down*. The content of a written communication is not only publicly accessible and objectively verifiable; it's also preserved for future generations. In theory, a message from God could be memorized by people and transmitted orally, without ever being committed to writing. But clearly that's not as effective in the long run as a written record. Consider for example the U.S. Constitution, one of the most important documents in American history. The words of the Constitution *could* have been preserved in memories and transmitted orally, but we understand very well why it was written down and why so many copies of it have been made. What applies to the words of the Founding Fathers surely applies all the more to the words of the Heavenly Father.

So then, if it's reasonable to believe in God, it's also eminently reasonable to believe that there are *divine scriptures*: written records of God's verbal communications to us.

WHERE HAS GOD SPOKEN?

I've argued that if there is a personal creator God, we should expect God to speak to us: indeed, to have *already* spoken to us. So the next question to ask is: *Where has God spoken?* Where do we find this communication from God?

I've explained why we should expect to find such a communication available in a written form, as publicly available scriptures. So those divinely inspired writings must be out there *somewhere*. Immediately, however, we run up against a problem. There are literally hundreds of religions in the world, many of them claiming to have their own divinely inspired scriptures. Since these various scriptures make conflicting claims—the Quran, for example, contradicts the Bible's teaching that Jesus was the Son of God—we have to discriminate between them. Which of all these writings are the *truly* inspired ones? When we consider all the possible candidates, it can strike us as quite overwhelming.

Once we start to survey the field, however, we can see that things aren't nearly as complex as they might first seem. The number of *serious* contenders turns out to be very small indeed. Any genuine divine revelation would have to fit a certain profile. Just as a work by Plato, Shakespeare, or Charles Dickens would have distinctive features reflecting its authorship, so any divinely authored writings would also have certain recognizable qualities.

We saw in the previous chapter that only a God who is transcendent, perfect and personal can account for the things we take for granted in our lives. So a *genuine* divine revelation would have to present itself as a verbal communication from *that* God. That immediately rules out the sacred scriptures of Eastern religions such as Hinduism, Jainism, Sikhism and Buddhism, since those writings don't present themselves as verbal revelations from a transcendent, perfect, personal God. (Of course, they may still contain much truth and wisdom; the point is that they don't fit the profile of a verbal communication from God, and they don't correctly depict God as transcendent, absolute and personal.)

The only major religions with scriptures that present themselves as verbal communications from God are the so-called 'Abrahamic' religions: Christianity, Islam and

Judaism. Only these religions affirm everything we've established so far: (1) God is the transcendent, absolute, personal Creator of the universe; (2) God has spoken to us; and (3) God's words have been preserved in sacred writings. However, these three religions disagree on *which* writings are divinely inspired. Judaism traditionally accepts only the *Tanakh*—the prophetic books written before the birth of Jesus, which Christians refer to as the Old Testament. Christianity agrees with Judaism that the Old Testament is divinely inspired, but adds that the New Testament is *also* divinely inspired. In fact, the New Testament claims to be the proper fulfilment of the Old Testament. So Christianity affirms not only the Old Testament but also the New Testament, the latter being written as a witness to Jesus' life, death and resurrection, and the birth of the Christian church.

How does Islam enter the debate? Here things get a little more complicated. Muslims believe that the Quran is a message from God which was delivered through the prophet Muhammad in the early seventh century (i.e. nearly 600 years after Jesus). However, Islam also teaches that the Quran isn't the only divine revelation in history and that Muhammad wasn't the only true prophet. Rather, Muhammad was the last in a series of prophets, and God delivered *earlier* revelations through a number of those prophets. Those scriptures include the *Tawrat* and the *Injil*, given through the prophets Moses and Jesus, respectively.[2] Muslims will add, however, that these earlier scriptures have become corrupted. Only the Quran is an uncorrupted and reliable divine revelation.

How can we navigate our way through this debate? How should we decide between these competing claims about where God has spoken? Once again, it will help to look at things from a worldview perspective. Christianity, Islam and Judaism represent three different worldviews, each with its own understanding of who God is, what God is like, and how God has spoken to us. So we can apply to each one the worldview tests discussed in chapter 2. Here I want to focus in particular on the *coherence* test. Which worldview best fits together internally?

Let's compare Judaism and Christianity first. Judaism accepts the Old Testament but rejects the New Testament. The problem, however, is that the Old Testament appears to be incomplete as it stands. It contains many promises and prophecies, the most striking of which concern a servant-king who would be sent by God to bring salvation to people from all nations of the world, whom the Jews came to refer to as 'the

---

2.   *Quran* 3:3; 5:43-48; 5:65-68. *Tawrat* is the Arabic form of Torah, referring to the first five books of the Old Testament. *Injil* is Arabic for Gospel.

Messiah' (literally, 'the Anointed One').[3] Yet we don't find these messianic promises and prophecies fulfilled in the Old Testament itself. They're just left hanging. As a friend of mine once put it, the Old Testament is like a half-built bridge. It goes up from one side but doesn't come down on the other! So the Old Testament raises the question: Where's the completion? Where's the fulfilment? *Where's the other half of the bridge?*

Christianity offers a clear and compelling answer: Jesus of Nazareth is the fulfilment of all these promises and prophecies.[4] The history of Israel, recorded in the books of the Old Testament, demonstrated that even those who receive special blessings from God cannot save themselves from their own moral corruption. They needed God to send a perfect savior to make a perfect atonement for their many acts of rebellion and idolatry. The life and death of Jesus of Nazareth, recorded in the books of the New Testament, presents the resolution to

---

3. The messianic themes are found in many Old Testament books, but most prominently in the book of Isaiah: 9:1-7; 11:1-10; 42:1-4; 52:13-53:12; 61:1-11. For a good overview of how these themes are developed in the Bible, see T. D. Alexander, *The Servant King: The Bible's Portrait of the Messiah* (InterVarsity Press, 1998).

4. This is one of the central themes of the New Testament book of Acts, which records the birth of the Christian church and the preaching of Jesus' earliest disciples. 'Christ' is the Greek form of the Jewish title 'Messiah'—hence 'Jesus Christ' simply means 'Jesus the Messiah'.

the problem spelled out at length in the Old Testament. So the two 'halves' of the Bible, the Old and New Testaments, fit together hand-in-glove.

- Prophecies—and fulfilments.
- Problem—and solution.
- Promises made—and promises kept.

What I'm suggesting then is that Christianity's answer to the question, 'Where has God spoken?' is more coherent than Judaism's answer, simply because it is more *complete*. The Old Testament without the New Testament is like a jigsaw puzzle with half of the pieces missing. You can't get the full picture!

Since modern Judaism denies that Jesus really was the promised Messiah, it's left with a gaping question: If not Jesus, *then who?* It stretches credibility to believe that someone else will appear who *better* fulfils all the promises and prophecies in the Jewish scriptures.

Let's turn now to compare Islam and Christianity. How do their respective claims about divine revelation compare? As I noted, the Quran doesn't purport to be the only communication from God. It actually affirms *parts* of the Bible as earlier scriptures given through divinely appointed prophets such as Moses and Jesus. In fact, if you read the Quran for yourself—and I recommend that you do—you'll discover that it leans heavily on the Bible.

A multitude of biblical stories and characters feature in the Quran, although often the details and the emphases have been changed so as to support the central message of the Quran, which can be summarized quite simply: repent of idolatry and immorality, acknowledge that there is only one true God, and submit absolutely to the will of God revealed through his prophet Muhammad.

I suggest there are a number of reasons to doubt the claims of the Quran to be a genuine divine revelation. For example, not only does the Quran reject the Christian doctrine of the Trinity, it also misrepresents that doctrine when it does so. It implies that Christians actually worship *three separate gods*—Allah, Jesus and Mary, the mother of Jesus—rather than one God who exists in *three distinct persons*—Father, Son and Holy Spirit.[5] The problem here is not that the Quran *disagrees* with what Christians believe, but rather that the God of the Quran should at least know what Christians actually believe in the first place. It's one thing for the Quran to say that what Christianity teaches is mistaken; it's quite another for the Quran to be mistaken about what Christianity actually teaches.

There are other examples of the Quran misrepresenting Christianity, but I want to focus here again on the

---

5. *Quran* 5:72-73 and 5:116. See also 4:171.

question of *coherence*. When it comes to claims about divine revelation, does the Islamic worldview cohere as well as the Christian worldview? The basic problem for Islam is that the Quran *affirms* earlier scriptures while also *contradicting* those same scriptures. The Quran says that the Torah was given by God to the Jews, yet it contradicts the Torah in a number of places.[6] It also speaks about 'the Gospel' given to Christians through Jesus, but it flatly contradicts some of the central claims made about Jesus in the Gospels of the New Testament. For example, the Quran denies that Jesus claimed to be the Son of God and that Jesus died by crucifixion as an atoning sacrifice for our sins.[7]

Now to be fair, Muslims have a ready answer to these objections. They contend that the earlier scriptures were *changed* by Jews and Christians. That's why these conflicts exist. The earlier scriptures have become corrupted, and therefore cannot be trusted. Leaving aside the question of *why* Jews and Christians would want to change scriptures which they believed to be God-given, this common Muslim answer actually raises more problems than it solves. In the first place, the Quran not only acknowledges the earlier scriptures, it encourages Jews and Christians

---

6. For example, the Quran says that one of Noah's sons drowned in the Great Flood (*Quran* 11:42-43).

7. *Quran* 4:157-158; 4:171; 5:72-75; 5:116-117; 112:1-4.

to *consult* those scriptures to confirm Muhammad's own message, which implies of course that those scriptures weren't corrupted in Muhammad's day.[8] That's a big problem, because we have physical manuscripts of the Old and New Testaments which have been reliably dated to hundreds of years *before* Muhammad's birth. These manuscripts prove that the Bible we have today is the same as the Bible that Christians had when the Quran was written. So it's hard to reconcile the idea that the Bible has been corrupted with what the Quran actually says and apparently takes for granted.

To compound the problem, the Quran insists in several places that God's words cannot be changed or corrupted.[9] Yet the earlier scriptures, such as the *Tawrat* and the *Injil*, are supposed to have been delivered by God in the same way as the Quran: received through a prophet and then preserved in written form. Muslims will insist that the Quran hasn't been changed since it was first received. Indeed, they'll say it *couldn't* be changed, because (as the Quran says) God wouldn't allow it. If God is so committed to preserving these later scriptures, why didn't He preserve the earlier scriptures too? Or to put the point in reverse: if God allowed the earlier scriptures to be corrupted so badly that they now can't be trusted,

---

8. *Quran* 3:3; 5:46-48; 5:65-68; 7:157; 10:94; 16:43-44; 21:7.

9. *Quran* 6:34; 6:114-115; 10:64; 15:9; 18:27.

what assurance does anyone have that the Quran hasn't also been corrupted? You can't throw the Bible under the bus without the Quran being dragged along with it.

So here's the argument in a nutshell: Christianity and Islam both teach that God has spoken to us through inspired scriptures, and those scriptures were given through a series of prophets over a long period of time. Both affirm that there were *earlier* and *later* scriptures: Christianity identifies those scriptures as the Old Testament and the New Testament, while Islam identifies them as *parts* of the Jewish and Christian scriptures, plus the Quran as the final revelation. Christianity teaches that all the scriptures God provided He has also preserved over the centuries, and those scriptures form a coherent whole: a story of redemption which centers on Jesus. In contrast, Islam has to maintain that *all the scriptures except the last* have been irremediably corrupted and lost. For some reason, God chose to preserve only the Quran, a book whose teachings deviate at major points from those of the Bible. What's more, we know that the Bible we have today is the very same Bible that Christians had in Muhammad's day.

In sum, when it comes to claims about what God is like and how God has revealed Himself over the course of human history, the Christian worldview is more internally coherent and consistent with the evidence than its two major competitors, Judaism and Islam. Once we recognize that God *would* speak to us, and we ask the question, '*Where* has God spoken?' the most reasonable answer by far is that God has spoken in the Old and New Testaments of the Bible. In fact, when we look at the alternatives offered by non-Christian worldviews, it turns out to be the *only* reasonable answer.[10]

ASK AN EXPERT

In the previous chapter I explained why you should believe in God—indeed, why in an important sense you *already* believe in God, whether you recognize it or not. In this chapter I've argued that you should also believe God has spoken to us in the Bible. Before I move on to discuss other elements of the Christian worldview, I want to come at the issue of the Bible from a slightly different but complementary perspective.

---

10. One issue I haven't addressed here is the question of the 'biblical canon' (basically, the 'table of contents' for the Bible). Who decided which books ended up in the Bible and on what basis? How do we know that the Bible contains all the right books? On one level, the answer is very simple: if God has provided inspired scriptures, He will also ensure that those scriptures are properly recognized and preserved. The historical details of that process, however, are rather complicated. For an excellent explanation of how the New Testament came together, see Michael J. Kruger, *Canon Revisited* (Crossway, 2012). As for the Old Testament, there was basically a consensus about the Jewish scriptures in Jesus' day. Christians therefore agree with Jews (more precisely, with Jesus!) that the books of the Old Testament are divinely inspired scriptures.

Perhaps you're familiar with the popular TV show *Who Wants to Be a Millionaire?* One of the features of the show is to offer contestants three 'lifelines' as they progress through the increasingly challenging questions: '50:50', 'Ask the Audience' and 'Phone a Friend'.

The '50:50' option reduces the choice of possible answers from four to two. 'Ask the Audience' invites the studio audience to select which of the possible answers they think is the correct one, and the contestant can then be guided by the majority vote. 'Phone a Friend' allows the contestant to seek the advice of one of a pre-selected pool of friends, presumably the one most likely to know the answer to the question.

The questions posed on *Who Wants to Be a Millionaire?* are literally *trivia* questions: items of general knowledge with little if any eternal significance. In contrast, the questions 'Has God spoken?' and 'Where has God spoken?' must be among the most important questions a person can ask. So if you could phone a friend for advice, which of your friends would you call?

Perhaps no one immediately springs to mind. But since this is such an important question, let's expand the pool. If you could ask *anyone in the history of the world*, who would it be? Who do you think would have the greatest insight and expertise on the question of knowing God? Who would you regard as most reliable and trustworthy—as the person most likely to know the answer?

I suggest that when we consider all the people who have lived in history, there is really only one obvious answer: *Jesus*. No one else comes close to Jesus in terms of moral character, spiritual insight and positive influence in the world. If *anyone* had a direct line to God, Jesus did.[11]

Now I'm sure you're thinking, 'Of course you'd say that—you're a Christian!' And you'd have a point. But I'd reply that even non-Christians can recognize that Jesus was a truly unique individual. Even those who don't accept Christianity can agree that Jesus' teachings are profound and worthy of consideration.

So how would Jesus answer the question before us? We don't need to speculate here, because every historical record we have about Jesus provides a clear and consistent answer. If we know anything at all about Jesus, we know that He believed and taught that the Old Testament scriptures were 'the word of God'.[12] He took for granted that those scriptures carried the authority of God. Remarkably, however, Jesus put His *own* teachings on the same level as the Old Testament scriptures, and

---

11. I realize Muslims will be inclined to answer 'Muhammad'! But remember that according to the Quran, Jesus was no less a prophet than Muhammad. So Muslims ought to accept Jesus' 'expert answer' here.

12. Matthew 4:4; 15:6; John 10:35.

He taught that He was the *fulfilment* of those scriptures.[13] He presented Himself as the promised Messiah of whom the prophets spoke.

Even though the New Testament hadn't yet been written when Jesus was teaching these things about Himself, He implicitly affirmed the bond between the Old and New Testaments, because the New Testament is nothing less than the record of Jesus' life and an explanation of how He fulfilled the Old Testament promises and prophecies, written at His instruction by His chosen disciples. All this is to say, if you could ask Jesus the question, 'Where has God spoken?' His answer would be short and simple: 'God has spoken in the Bible.'

That's certainly consistent with the Christian world-view. But it's not the whole story, because it's not the whole answer. For if you were standing in front of Jesus, asking the question, 'Where has God spoken?' you might just as well hear this answer from Him:

'God is speaking to you *right here and right now*.'

And that immediately leads us to another worldview-defining question, which will be our focus in the next chapter: *Who is Jesus?*

---

13. Matthew 26:54, 56; Luke 4:16-21; 24:25-27, 44-47; John 5:39.

6

God With Us

'Who is John Galt?'

The question posed in the opening line of Ayn Rand's novel *Atlas Shrugged*, and repeated throughout the book, doesn't receive an answer until the final third of the novel where the identity of John Galt is eventually revealed. Rand's novel is much admired in some circles, but if you don't know who John Galt is, you needn't lose any sleep over it. Galt's identity matters to the plot of the novel, of course, but he's a fictional character and his identity has little if any bearing on our everyday lives.

The same cannot be said for the question, 'Who is Jesus?' Among mainstream historians there's no question that Jesus of Nazareth was a real person, a Jewish teacher who lived in the first half of the first century A.D. In fact, the abbreviation I just used—A.D.—underscores the point. Our Western calendar takes for granted that Jesus was a real historical individual. Not just any individual, indeed, but one with such enormous significance that an entire civilization would center its dating system on His birth.

In an earlier chapter I said that a worldview addresses the 'big questions' of human existence, such as whether God exists, what God is like, where we came from, and what is the purpose of our lives. I want to suggest that the true identity of Jesus of Nazareth is one of those 'big questions', a question of such immense import that how you answer it should affect your entire perspective on life and your own existence. Of course, that's not to deny there are other people in history who have shaped our worldviews: Moses, Muhammad, the Buddha, Karl Marx and Charles Darwin, to list but a few examples. But even people who aren't Christians recognize the remarkable significance of Jesus and His impact on the course of human history. Christianity, Islam and Judaism all take a distinctive position on who Jesus was, and adherents of Eastern religions often want to acknowledge His spiritual significance as well. No other religious figure made pronouncements on a par with those of Jesus, and His astonishing claims need to be taken seriously. Whether you believe what Jesus taught about Himself—about who He was and what He came to do—will have enormous implications for how you view yourself and the world.

So who was Jesus of Nazareth? There's no shortage of answers to the question. Islam claims that Jesus was a divinely appointed prophet, but just one in a line of prophets that ended with Muhammad. While Islam views Jesus as a true prophet, traditional Judaism says in effect that Jesus was a *false* prophet. He claimed to be the Messiah foretold by the prophets of the Old Testament, but He taught things about Himself that were tantamount to blasphemy and eventually led to His death. That said, many Jews today would say that Jesus was a good man and that some of His teachings reflect genuine spiritual wisdom and virtue, even though His other teachings were false and overblown.

Adherents of Eastern religions such as Hinduism and Buddhism often have a high regard for Jesus, viewing Him as something like a spiritual guru who was especially in touch with the divine and who taught others how to attain peace and enlightenment. It's an attractive idea for many people, but the reality is that Jesus' teachings need to be radically reinterpreted in order to make them fit with the worldviews of these Eastern religions. As I noted at the end of the previous chapter, Jesus affirmed the authority of the Old Testament scriptures, and His teachings assume the *worldview* of those scriptures, a worldview in which there is a transcendent, holy, personal, creator God who is distinct from His creation. That outlook is wholly at odds with Eastern worldviews, which tend to blur the distinction between God and the universe. None of Jesus' Jewish contemporaries would have viewed Him as a spiritual guru who was pointing to 'the divine within each one of us'.

Non-religious people also have various views on Jesus. Many consider Him essentially a good man who offered some admirable moral teachings and showed great love towards His fellow human beings, but who was also a product of His time and culture. So they'd say that Jesus' beliefs about God and the afterlife are naïve and outdated in light of our modern scientific knowledge. Others, such as the atheist philosopher Bertrand Russell, go further and say that Jesus really wasn't such a good person after all; they regard some of His teachings as immoral, delusional and just plain dangerous. A fringe minority of skeptics have gone so far as to propose that Jesus never actually existed—a position that no respectable historian (Christian or otherwise) takes seriously. But even that extreme skeptical view underscores my point: *whoever* Jesus was, He cannot be simply ignored. If Jesus isn't all that important, why would some people go to such great lengths to disprove His existence?

THE CHRISTIAN VIEW OF JESUS

While it's interesting to consider how Jesus has been viewed by non-Christians, the focus of this book is Christianity. So in this chapter I will summarize the Christian view of Jesus and explain why it's reasonable to believe what Christians believe about Jesus. One of the earliest statements of Christian beliefs, the Apostles' Creed, says the following:

> I believe in God the Father Almighty, Maker of heaven and earth. I believe in Jesus Christ, his only Son, our Lord, who was conceived by the Holy Spirit, and born of the virgin Mary. He suffered under Pontius Pilate, was crucified, died, and was buried; he descended into hell. The third day he rose again from the dead. He ascended into heaven and is seated at the right hand of God the Father Almighty. From there he will come to judge the living and the dead.

On the one hand, the creed affirms that Jesus was a real, historical, flesh-and-blood human being. He was conceived and born. He suffered and died. But the creed also reflects the Christian conviction that Jesus wasn't *merely* a human being. He was also, uniquely, the Son of God.

A later Christian confession, the Nicene Creed, states more precisely what it means for Jesus to be the Son of God. It doesn't mean merely that Jesus has a special relationship with God or a special role within

God's plans. No, it means something infinitely more profound: Jesus is actually *divine*. Just as a human son shares the nature of his father—both are essentially *human*, even though they're distinct persons—so the Son of God shares the nature of His Father. Both the Father and the Son are essentially *divine*, even though they're distinct persons.

This conviction about the divinity of Jesus wasn't a late development in the history of Christianity, as some modern scholars have claimed. As I'll show in this chapter, it's firmly rooted in the claims of Jesus' first disciples—indeed, in Jesus' own teachings. But before we get to that, it's worth taking a moment to consider how this view of Jesus' true identity fits into the broader Christian worldview.

WHY DID GOD BECOME MAN?

I've noted a number of times that one of the virtues a worldview can exhibit is *coherence*, that is, the degree to which its basic tenets support and explain one another. When a worldview is coherent we can make observations like this: 'Given that this worldview affirms A, B and C, it makes sense that it also affirms D, E and F.' Christianity's claims about the divinity of Jesus offer an excellent example of the coherence of the Christian worldview and its basic storyline.

At the center of the Christian worldview is its view of God: the transcendent, all-glorious Creator of the universe. God created the universe out of nothing by His unlimited power. He made a universe with an incredible diversity of life, the pinnacle of which is *human* life.[1] God created us 'in His own image' to enjoy a personal relationship with Him. Yet we have rebelled against Him and brought divine judgment upon ourselves. Since God is the author of life, and we owe our very existence to Him, the just punishment for rebellion against God is death. All of us deserve the divine death penalty for our violation of God's perfect moral laws. That's the bad news.

God's goodness, however, is multifaceted. It's expressed in His mercy as well as His justice. Christianity proclaims the good news that God has provided a way for rebels like us to be reconciled to God. But how can the chasm between a holy God and unholy humans be bridged? In order for two parties to be reconciled, there needs to be a *mediator*: someone who can 'stand in the middle' and represent both parties. The central message of the Bible is that God Himself has provided a perfect

---

1. 'You have made [human beings] a little lower than the angels and crowned them with glory and honor. You made them rulers over the works of your hands; you put everything under their feet.' (Psalm 8:5-6)

mediator: Jesus Christ.[2] But in order to be a mediator between us and God, Jesus would have to be *both* human *and* divine. He would have to be human in order to represent the human race before the Divine Judge. Yet He would also have to be divine, because no one but God could have the authority to represent God. Jesus the God-man, the divine-human bridge, was uniquely qualified to be the Savior of the fallen human race.

The coherence of the Christian worldview gives us a preliminary reason to believe Christianity's claim about the divinity of Jesus. If it's reasonable to believe there is a transcendent, holy, personal God, it's also reasonable to believe we're under His judgment. After all, God is absolutely perfect in goodness, and we are far from good in many ways. It's normal human experience to sense this moral failure and guilt before God. But because God's goodness includes compassion and mercy as well as holiness and justice, it's reasonable to believe God has provided some way for us to escape the terrifying prospect of divine judgment. That deliverance would require some kind of *atonement*, an act that cancels out the sin which has broken our relationship with God. If the just penalty for rebellion against God is death, then *someone* has to satisfy that penalty on our behalf. But our

---

2. 1 Timothy 2:5-6.

dire predicament means that we can't make atonement for ourselves, precisely because everything we do is tainted with moral failure. If we had to make our own atonement, we'd still need someone else to atone for all our flawed attempts to make our own atonement!

The only person who could make an adequate atonement would be a person who is *both human and divine*. Human, so that He could suffer the penalty of death on our behalf. Divine, so that His life would be absolutely flawless and His sacrifice would be sufficiently valuable to pay the price, not merely for one other human life but for *any number* of human lives. The problem of human sin requires a solution that fits the problem. Jesus, as the perfect God-man, represents the *perfect* sacrifice for sin. I trust you can see that what Christianity claims about the basic human problem, and what it claims about Jesus as the solution to that problem, go together hand-in-glove.

'WHO DO YOU SAY I AM?'

The question of the true identity of Jesus isn't a modern question, of course. It was the question asked by many people who encountered Jesus personally. Indeed, in a fascinating exchange recorded in Matthew's Gospel, Jesus posed that very question to His own disciples:

> When Jesus came to the region of Caesarea Philippi, he asked his disciples, 'Who do people say the Son of

> Man is?' They replied, 'Some say John the Baptist;
> others say Elijah; and still others, Jeremiah or one
> of the prophets.' 'But what about you?' he asked.
> 'Who do you say I am?' Simon Peter answered,
> 'You are the Messiah, the Son of the living God.'[3]

Evidently Jesus had stirred up a lot of debate and various theories about His identity were doing the rounds. Yet His own disciples were quite clear on who Jesus was. He was the Messiah promised in the Old Testament scriptures, the Savior sent by God—but even more than that, Jesus was 'the Son of the living God'.

The title 'Son of God' is exalted enough as it is. Over time, however, the disciples came to see its full implications: the Son of God is *equal with God*. This becomes most evident in John's Gospel, the last of the four accounts of Jesus' life to be written, and from the pen of one of Jesus' own disciples.[4] In the introduction to his account, John refers to Jesus as 'the Word' (probably to convey the idea that Jesus is God's self-revelation) and the way he describes Jesus is quite staggering:

> In the beginning was the Word, and the Word was
> with God, and the Word was God. He was with
> God in the beginning. Through him all things
> were made; without him nothing was made that
> has been made.[5]

---

3.   Matthew 16:13-16.

4.   John 21:20-24.

5.   John 1:1-3.

The Word—the Son of God—existed from the very beginning. On the one hand, He was *with* God, and yet at the very same time, He *was* God! Although the word 'Trinity' isn't found in the New Testament, this is one of the places where the idea of the Trinity is expressed most strikingly. There is one and only one God. (Remember that the first Christians, including John, were Jewish monotheists.) Even so, there are *personal distinctions* within the one God—in this case, a distinction between the Father and the Son. As if to leave us in no doubt that the Word is equal with God, John adds that everything that has been made—that is, everything in the creation— was made *through* Him. So the Word cannot be *part* of the creation.

Since John makes such exalted claims about 'the Word', you might be wondering whether we know for sure that he's referring to Jesus. To confirm it, we need only to continue reading John's introduction until we reach the following statements:

> The Word became flesh and made his dwelling among us. We have seen his glory, the glory of the one and only Son, who came from the Father, full of grace and truth.[6]

---

6. John 1:14. See also verses 17-18 of the same chapter, where John directly refers to Jesus as 'God' while also distinguishing Him from 'the Father'.

There really can be no doubt that John, who knew Jesus personally, had come to the startling conclusion that Jesus was a divine person who had taken on a human nature in order to save us. And John wasn't an outlier here. There isn't the slightest indication in the New Testament that any of the other disciples took a lower view of Jesus. The apostle Paul, who wasn't one of the original twelve disciples but experienced a dramatic conversion when (according to his own testimony) he encountered Jesus alive after His crucifixion, expressed the same high view of Jesus. Consider what he wrote in a letter to fellow Christians in the city of Philippi:

> In your relationships with one another, have the same mindset as Christ Jesus: Who, **being in very nature God**, did not consider equality with God something to be used to his own advantage; rather, he made himself nothing **by taking the very nature of a servant, being made in human likeness**. And being found in appearance as a man, he humbled himself by becoming obedient to death—even death on a cross! Therefore God exalted him to the highest place and gave him the name that is above every name, that at the name of Jesus every knee should bow, in heaven and on earth and under the earth, and every tongue acknowledge that Jesus Christ is Lord, to the glory of God the Father.[7]

---

7. Philippians 2:5-11. What's so remarkable about this passage is that Paul directly applies to Jesus language about God from the Old Testament (see Isaiah 45:22-25).

Paul expresses here the same convictions as John: Jesus, the Son of God, had *the very nature of God*, yet He took on a human nature so that He could die for our sins. In another of his letters, Paul echoes John's statement that everything was created *through* the Son of God (which means, of course, that the Son of God Himself is on the Creator side of the divide, not the creation side) and adds that 'the fullness of God' dwelled in Jesus Christ.[8] Many other verses in the New Testament could be added to show that Jesus' followers believed He had existed eternally and was equal with the Creator of the universe.

'That's all very interesting,' you may say, 'but people believed lots of strange things back then. Why should we give their beliefs any credit?' It's crucial to recognize just how surprising and unlikely these beliefs about Jesus were *even for those people*. Jesus' disciples were first-century Jewish monotheists. They believed in a transcendent, personal God who created the universe out of nothing, and they treated with utmost seriousness the Old Testament commandment to worship and serve *only* God.[9] Given their worldview, they were predisposed to agree with Jesus' critics that it was blasphemous for any human to claim equality with God. Yet their encounters with Jesus led them to the incredible conclusion that

---

8.   Colossians 1:15-17 & 2:9-10.

9.   Exodus 20:3 & 34:14; Deuteronomy 6:13-15 & 8:19.

Jesus really *was* the divine Son of God. Indeed, they came to the point where they were willing to *worship* Him.[10] That so many devout first-century Jews became worshippers of a fellow human being begs for a satisfying explanation. We cannot help but ask: *What was it about Jesus that convinced them?*

WHO DID HE SAY HE WAS?

Skeptics will often insist that the idea of Jesus' divinity was a late development, and that Jesus Himself never made such outlandish claims. As we've seen, however, Jesus' earliest followers, many of whom had lived with Him for years, believed that He was equal with God. It would be very strange for that to happen if Jesus Himself had given no hint of that! In reality, however, Jesus' own teachings about His true identity and authority point consistently in the same direction.

People who say that Jesus never claimed to be God tend to fall into one of two camps: those who haven't actually studied the four Gospels for themselves, and those who assume that if Jesus really thought He was divine then He would have said so in the most explicit and unambiguous terms: 'I'm God!' Or perhaps even: 'I'm the second person of the divine Trinity. Nice to meet you!'

---

10. Matthew 14:33; 28:9, 17; Luke 24:52; John 9:38.

It takes only a moment's reflection to see that it would have been very counter-productive for Jesus to have spoken in those terms. We have to remember that Jesus was a first-century Jew, preaching to other first-century Jews, all of whom were strict monotheists who believed fervently in the transcendence and holiness of God. Someone who baldly declared 'I'm God!' would have been dismissed by everyone as a blasphemous lunatic from the very outset. Nothing else he said would be taken seriously. Moreover, for Jesus to refer to Himself as 'God' would have obscured the distinction between the Father and the Son. (Bear in mind that at this point in history the New Testament, which fully reveals God's Trinitarian nature, had not yet been written.) As we'll see, some of Jesus' contemporaries did indeed accuse Him of blasphemy, but Jesus wisely adopted a more indirect approach to disclosing His true identity, one that forced people to consider His claims more carefully.

It's essential to recognize that Jesus had many other things to teach people than simply, 'I'm God.' His message was one of good news—and if you're an ungodly sinner, hearing someone claim to be God hardly counts as good news! Jesus had much more to say about who He was and what He had come to do. Nevertheless, what He *did* say about Himself, when understood against the backdrop of the Old Testament, certainly implied that He was much more than a mere human being. So let's examine some of those statements.

There's really no doubt that Jesus claimed to be the promised Messiah and the Son of God. When Peter replied to His question, 'Who do you say I am?' with the answer, 'You are the Messiah, the Son of the living God', Jesus commended him for his answer:

> 'Blessed are you, Simon son of Jonah, for this was not revealed to you by flesh and blood, but by my Father in heaven.'[11]

Many times in the Gospels we find Jesus referred to as 'the Son of God' by others, and not once did He indicate that it was inappropriate.[12] In fact, Jesus used the title Himself on occasions, and at other times He referred to Himself as 'the Son' in contexts where it's clear He meant 'the Son of God'.[13] It's important to recognize that Jesus treated this title as one that applied *uniquely* to Him. It's not as though Jesus was only calling Himself *a* son of God—as if other folk could be a son or daughter of God in the same sense. He claimed to have a one-of-a-kind

11. Matthew 16:17.

12. Matthew 8:29; 14:33; 27:43; Luke 22:70; John 1:34, 49; 11:27; 19:7.

13. Matthew 11:27; 16:27; 24:36; 28:19; Mark 8:38; 12:1-2; 14:60-64; John 5:25; 10:36; 11:4.

relationship with God the Father—one that preceded even His human birth.[14]

Even more provocative were some of the other things Jesus said. He claimed to have the authority to forgive other people's sins, a claim His critics considered to have blasphemous implications, because the Jews believed that only God has the right to pardon sin.[15] On one occasion Jesus declared Himself to be 'the Lord of the Sabbath', which would have sounded scandalous to a Jew, since 'Lord' was the primary designation for God in the Old Testament, and the Sabbath commandment had been given by God.[16] Ask any first-century Jew, 'Who is the Lord of the Sabbath?' and without hesitation he would have replied: 'God!'

Those are just two examples of Jesus claiming to have authority that put Him on a par with God. Other examples could be cited, but perhaps the most all-encompassing statement came at the very end of Jesus' ministry, when He claimed to have 'all authority in heaven and on earth.'[17] How else could that be interpreted but as a claim to have *divine* authority? Did Jesus think God

---

14. John 8:58; 17:5.

15. Mark 2:1-12.

16. Mark 2:23-28. The Sabbath commandment appears in Exodus 20:8-11.

17. Matthew 28:18.

could somehow abdicate His authority over the universe and give it to one of His creatures?

John's Gospel makes particularly clear the implications of Jesus' outrageous claims. Jesus' enemies recognized that calling Himself the Son of God was tantamount to claiming equality with God, and so they sought to have Him killed for blasphemy.[18] On another occasion Jesus stated quite brazenly, 'I and the Father are one,' and His opponents responded by picking up stones in order to stone Him to death. They were quite clear about their justification: It was 'for blasphemy, because you, a mere man, claim to be God.'[19] Another time, Jesus made the astonishing claim that He had existed even before Abraham was born, and went as far as to apply the divine name 'I AM' to Himself.[20] Can you guess how people responded to that one? (Hint: stones were involved again.)

I've hardly scratched the surface here of the evidence for Jesus claiming to be God. But even a cursory examination of His words and actions reveals that Jesus more than encouraged the idea that He was divine. Let

---

18. John 5:18.

19. John 10:30-33. Compare Mark 14:60-64, where the Jewish high priest charges Jesus with blasphemy for claiming to be 'the Messiah, the Son of the Blessed One' (i.e. the Son of God).

20. John 8:58; Exodus 3:14.

me put it this way: If Jesus *didn't* want people to think He was divine, He has to go down as one of the worst teachers in the history of the world!

Of course, just because someone *claims* to be divine, it doesn't follow that he *is* divine. Jesus wasn't the first person to claim to be divine, nor was He the last. There are plenty of people alive today who make similar claims, and most of them are being treated for mental illness. But that's precisely the point, isn't it? It's not simply that Jesus said He was the divine Son of God. It's that hundreds of people who knew Him *believed Him*. Jesus gave absolutely no indication of being deranged or trying to dupe people. If Jesus honestly took Himself to be a divine person who had existed with God the Father from eternity, He must have had some serious reason to believe such an incredible notion. And His disciples must have had good reason to believe it too.

When we put it in the context of everything else we know about His character and His actions, Jesus' own testimony about His identity gives us good reason to believe that He really was more than just a human prophet, a spiritual guru, or a superlative moral example.

Confirming Evidence

From a Christian perspective, Jesus' own testimony is evidence enough. After all, if that testimony is *true* then it carries the highest conceivable authority—the authority of God. As Jesus Himself indicated, it takes supernatural insight to recognize and accept His self-testimony.[21] Only the sheep will hear the voice of the shepherd.[22]

But for those who don't yet believe that Jesus is who He claimed to be, more needs to be said—and indeed more can be said. If Jesus really was the Son of God who became human for our salvation, as Christianity teaches, we would expect there to be further evidence consistent with that truth. I've already observed that the Christian view of God, and our standing before God as sinners in need of atonement, gives us initial reason to expect a divine incarnation. Furthermore, if Jesus really was the Son of God, we'd expect Him to make claims consistent with His divine identity, and we'd expect those who knew Him best to echo those claims. That's exactly what we find.

But what other evidence should we see? For one thing we should find that Jesus' *actions* demonstrate His divine character and power, corroborating His claims. Apparently not even His enemies could point to any moral failings in Him—other than blasphemously claiming equality with God! Jesus was also renowned in His day as a healer and miracle-worker. Here again, even

---

21. Matthew 16:17.
22. John 10:25-28.

His critics conceded that He had performed miracles. They just preferred to argue that His amazing powers came from Satan rather than God.[23] All this to say, Jesus' reputation among those who encountered Him, both friends and foes, supported His claim to be the Son of God.

To all of this we can also add the evidence of prophecy. Jesus' life fulfilled a host of prophecies in the Old Testament, many of which concerned the circumstances of His birth and His death—events which on the face of it were beyond Jesus' direct control. Yet a number of these prophecies also indicated that the promised Messiah would be more than a mere man. God *Himself* would come into the world to save His people.[24] So the fact that Jesus fit the profile of the Messiah provides further evidence of His true identity.

There's one other important piece of evidence for Jesus' divinity which at least needs to be mentioned here. Not only did Jesus' followers claim that He was the Son of God, they also claimed that He had risen from the dead. Perhaps surprisingly, the disciples never argued that Jesus' resurrection *proved* that Jesus was the Son of God, as if that had been in doubt before He died.

---

23. Matthew 12:22-32.

24. Psalm 45:6-7; Isaiah 7:14; 9:6-7; 40:3-5; Jeremiah 23:5-6; Daniel 7:13-14; Micah 5:2; Zechariah 12:10; Malachi 3:1.

But there's a connection nonetheless. Think it through for a moment. If Jesus had *falsely* claimed to be equal with God, and had been put to death on the charge of blasphemy, would God have raised Him from the dead? What message would a miraculous resurrection convey about Jesus' claims?

As I'm sure you'll point out, Jesus' resurrection can only be evidence of His true identity if it actually occurred. So hold that thought for now. We'll tackle the question of the resurrection head-on in the next chapter.

But Is It Even Possible?

At this point some readers may be thinking along these lines:

> That's all very interesting again, but it's really beside the point. There's a fundamental problem here: it's just plain *illogical* and *impossible* for God to become human. The idea of a God-man is no more logical than the idea of a square circle! How could the transcendent, immaterial, timeless God become a flesh-and-blood human in space and time? How could the omnipotent and omniscient Creator of the universe become a finite creature with all the limitations that would involve? This central tenet of the Christian worldview is inherently unreasonable. It defies reason!

Let me concede right away that this is a genuine concern which shouldn't be casually dismissed. Yet it's also one that Christianity has acknowledged from the outset. Christian theologians have long maintained that the doctrine of the Incarnation, like the doctrine of the Trinity, is very mysterious and paradoxical. That's not a concession that these doctrines are nonsensical or contrary to reason. Rather, it's an admission that these teachings, which come directly from the Bible, can only be *partially* understood by human reason. It's a mediating position: Christianity isn't irrational, but the full truth about God inevitably goes beyond what our intellects can accommodate, just as a thimble can contain only a fraction of the water poured out from a basin.

That being said, we can go some way toward showing that it isn't inherently unreasonable to believe that God can—and did—take on a human nature. In the first place, we need to be clear that Christianity doesn't teach that Jesus changed from one kind of being (divine) into another kind of being (human). Jesus didn't cease to be the Son of God when He became a man. God can't stop being God! Christians do believe, however, that God the Son—the second person of the Trinity—*added* a human nature to His divine nature, precisely so that He could suffer and die a human death in our place.

Admittedly it's very hard for us to understand *how* God could do that. But the mere fact that we don't know *how* something could happen doesn't entail that it *couldn't*

187

or *didn't* happen. Imagine an aborigine in the remote Australian outback who has never encountered modern electronic communication devices. You tell him that you have a little box which you can speak into, and tens of thousands of miles away, someone with another little box can hear you and speak back to you. He doesn't have the first idea *how* that is possible! But that's no good reason to think it *isn't* possible. Now reflect on the fact that the difference between the aborigine's knowledge and yours is truly negligible compared to the difference between your knowledge and God's. The admission that neither you nor I have the first idea *how* God could do something gives us no good reason to think God *couldn't* do it.[25]

It's worth noting also that perplexities like this one aren't unique to the Christian worldview. Every worldview has to concede mystery at points. The question is whether the worldview as a whole justifies accepting those mysteries. Furthermore, paradoxes are encountered not only in theology and philosophy but in science as well. Here's just one example: most scientists accept Einstein's relativity theories as well as quantum mechanics, but it's widely acknowledged that there's a conflict between these two areas of modern physics. According to Einstein's theories, it's impossible for

---

25. In fact, we can go further: if we have evidence that God *did* do it, we have reason to think God *can* do it!

a physical event in one location to affect a physical event in another location without *some* delay between the two events. Yet according to quantum mechanics that *can* happen—and experiments have been performed which seem to show that it *does* happen. Scientists have been struggling for decades to try to reconcile these two well-established physical theories. No one has yet come up with a satisfying solution. Nevertheless, scientists still think it's reasonable to accept these theories anyway, despite the paradoxes they present.

So the mysteriousness of the Christian doctrine of the Incarnation shouldn't be seen as a reason not to believe it. In fact, I would suggest that the opposite is true. If a transcendent God were to take on a human nature, wouldn't we *expect* that to be mysterious at some level? Wouldn't we expect it to go beyond what our limited minds can comprehend? The mystery of the Incarnation is arguably evidence of its truthfulness. When we reflect on it in the broader context of the Christian worldview, the Incarnation becomes more credible rather than less so.

7

Defying Death

'In this world nothing can be said to be certain,' wrote Benjamin Franklin, 'except death and taxes.' It's true that death and taxes are both inevitable, but there's also a big difference between the two. Taxes are avoidable—at least in principle! At best we can merely delay death. It comes to us all eventually.

The promise of immortality—the ambition to overcome death itself—has always had a grip on the human imagination. Numerous movies, such as *The Lost Boys*, *Indiana Jones and the Last Crusade* and *The Fountain*, have taken the prospect of immortality as a central theme. Sometimes immortality is presented in positive terms—but not always. Whether an endless life is a good thing will depend on the quality of that life. Even so, most people recognize that death in itself is a *bad thing*. It's a threat. It's an enemy. When a loved one faces the prospect of death, it pains us. When a loved one is claimed by death, we weep and mourn. When we consider the prospect of our own death, we find it sobering and fearful.

There are some people who actively seek death. But they don't do so because they think death itself is good. They do so either because they believe that a happier afterlife will follow death, or because they cannot cope with the pain of their current life. In the latter case, they choose death because it seems to be the only alternative. Surely they would choose life without pain, rather than no life at all, if they thought that option were open to them.

One of the most appealing aspects of Christianity is its teaching about life, death and life after death. According to the biblical Christian worldview, death isn't part of the original creation. God is the author of all life, including human life. The shadow of death that hangs over us is a consequence of our rebellion against God: it is the just penalty for our sin. The good news is that God has provided a solution through His Son, who became one of us so that He could suffer the penalty of death in our place. Jesus died—but He didn't *stay* dead. On the third day He rose from the dead and appeared alive to many people over the course of forty days before

He 'ascended into heaven'.[1] Jesus suffered death, but in doing so He *conquered* death—once and for all. Because He is the Lord of life, He has the power and the authority to give *eternal* life to those who trust in Him for salvation.

The implication for the rest of us is that Jesus' resurrection opens the door to *our* resurrection. In keeping with the Old Testament scriptures, Jesus taught that bodily death isn't the end of a human being. We aren't purely physical creatures. Our souls continue to exist after our bodies expire. But it's important to emphasize that the future hope of Christianity is *not* an ethereal, disembodied existence forevermore. Jesus declared that a day would come when every single person will be raised from the dead, when every soul will be reunited with a resurrected body. Yet that will not be a joyful day for all. Some will 'rise to live'—that is, to enjoy eternal life in the presence of God—while others will 'rise to be condemned'.[2]

The resurrection of Jesus is one of the most distinctive and essential teachings of Christianity. It was central to the message preached by the first Christians.[3] The apostle Paul stated frankly that if Jesus is still dead and buried

---

1. Acts 1:1-11.

2. John 5:28-29.

3. Acts 2:22-36; 3:12-15; 4:8-12; 5:29-32—and so on throughout the book of Acts!

then Christianity is worthless and Christians should be pitied for their false hope.[4] Put simply, Christianity stands or falls on its claim that Jesus rose from the dead—that His tomb is empty and He is alive even now.

Of course, that's a quite extraordinary claim. So why should anyone believe it?

HARD TO BELIEVE

Let's be honest. It's not easy to believe that a man who was publicly executed returned from the dead three days later. It sounds like a pitch for a Hollywood movie! It's a truly extraordinary claim. In any other circumstances, we'd think it wholly incredible that a dead man came back to life. The late skeptic Christopher Hitchens invited the audience at one of his public debates to imagine striking up a conversation with a stranger on a bus who nonchalantly remarks, 'You know, I used to be a dead person, but I'm alive now!' Hitchens observed that the most reasonable response to such a statement would be not to believe it, but to relocate to another seat.

The eighteenth-century Scottish Enlightenment philosopher David Hume was no less skeptical about the Christian doctrine of Christ's resurrection. He quipped that since a resurrection would fly in the face of all our past experience, it would actually take a miracle

---

4. 1 Corinthians 15:12-19.

for someone to believe that it happened. So why *do* Christians believe it?

The short answer is: *because the Bible says so*. As I explained in chapter 5, Christianity teaches that the Bible is divinely inspired and that the Spirit of God gives people the ability to perceive the voice of God speaking in the words of the Bible. One of the clearest and most central claims of the New Testament is that God raised Jesus from the dead. In a sense, Hume was absolutely right. It *does* take a supernatural work of God for someone to believe what the Bible says about Jesus' resurrection.

However, that doesn't mean Christians believe it on the basis of blind faith, without reason or evidence. On the contrary, the reports of Jesus' resurrection in the New Testament are grounded in credible eyewitness testimony. The four Gospels, and the various letters included in the New Testament, were written either by people who claimed to have seen Jesus alive following His crucifixion, or by people who personally knew such eyewitnesses. Those eyewitnesses were sufficiently trustworthy in their characters, diverse in their backgrounds, and consistent in their reports, that their claims have to be taken seriously. They had no incentive to lie about what took place after Jesus' death. They had nothing to gain from such a deception—and a great deal to lose.

But I suppose the question in your mind is not why

Christians believe that Jesus rose from the dead, but rather why *you* should believe it. In this chapter, I will make the case that despite what you may have assumed there are no good reasons *not* to believe in Jesus' resurrection and many good reasons to accept it. Once we understand it in the broader context of the Christian worldview, and we consider the various alternative theories about what happened to Jesus, the Christian claim that He was raised from the dead actually makes perfectly good sense.

The Possibility of Miracles

Let's begin by dealing with some of the main objections to the resurrection. Clearly if Jesus returned from the dead that would be a *miraculous* event. Resurrections aren't *natural* events. The natural course of events is for dead people to stay dead! So if the resurrection actually occurred, it would require a supernatural cause or explanation.[5]

Some people dismiss the claim that Jesus rose from the dead because they think miracles are impossible in principle. Miracles just *can't* happen. Every event has a natural cause. A miracle would violate the laws of nature, but the laws of nature can't be violated; if they

---

5. There are, of course, cases of people declared 'clinically dead' who have been resuscitated shortly afterwards, but none of these involve a person dead for several days.

could, they wouldn't be laws.

Such thinking is very common, but it's also very flawed. Laws aren't *by definition* inviolable. (Just think of the laws of logic, for example, which are regularly flouted.) Strictly speaking the laws of nature only describe how things proceed *naturally*—that is, how the natural universe behaves in *normal* circumstances. The laws of nature by definition don't tell us anything about *supernatural* causes. Furthermore, if the universe was indeed created by God, then God is the *author* of the laws of nature, which means God has the authority and the power to suspend or bypass those laws on occasions if it suits His purposes.

In other words, if there is a God who created this universe, then miracles *must* be possible. To insist that miracles are impossible is really to deny the existence of God. But as I've already argued, the most basic aspects of human existence don't make sense apart from the existence of God. Consequently, every reason to believe in God is also a reason to believe that miracles are possible: that things *can* happen which defy any purely natural explanation.

Ironically, for this reason the popular idea that miracles conflict with science has things backwards. Science is only possible because the universe is the creation of an orderly, rational, personal God. The same God who makes *science* possible also makes *miracles* possible. The same God who guarantees the orderliness of the natural universe can also intervene in the natural course of events if He wishes to do so. Miracles are neither impossible nor irrational. They aren't impossible, because God is unlimited in power. They aren't irrational, because God is perfect in wisdom: He would never bring about a miracle without a good reason. And as I'll argue shortly, God had excellent reasons to raise Jesus from the dead.

In reality, those who deny the possibility of miracles are dismissing the Christian worldview from the outset, without considering the actual evidence for it. They're simply taking for granted *another* worldview—most likely the worldview of Naturalism, according to which the universe is a closed system of purely natural (physical) causes. But as I explained in chapter 4, Naturalism is a self-defeating worldview on multiple fronts.

THE PROBABILITY OF A MIRACLE

Even if miracles are possible, it doesn't follow that it's reasonable to believe any bizarre miracle claim that happens to come our way. In fact, I think we ought to be generally skeptical about miracle claims. If there's a plausible natural explanation for some phenomenon, we should prefer that over a supernatural explanation. If miracles are to have any value at all, they must be truly exceptional.

However, some critics of Christianity have taken this

default skepticism a step further and argued that natural explanations should *always* be preferred, no matter what. They'll say something like this:

> Sure, no one can prove that miracles are *impossible*. Even so, miracles are by definition highly improbable. In fact, they're so enormously improbable that any non-miraculous alternative explanation for the evidence will be more probable, and therefore more reasonable to believe, than the supposed miracle.

There's some truth to this line of thought. Miracles are indeed very improbable events. If they weren't, they wouldn't be so interesting and important! But it's a mistake to think that miracles are so intrinsically improbable that it could *never* be reasonable to believe one had actually occurred.

To see this point, let's consider another kind of improbable event: winning the lottery. Suppose you have a friend, Alex, who plays the lottery every week. Let's assume that ten million tickets are sold this week, that Alex buys one ticket, and that every ticket has an equal chance of winning. So the odds of Alex winning the lottery this week are one in ten million. Obviously with those odds it's extremely improbable that Alex— not just anyone, but Alex specifically—will win the lottery.[6] It would be entirely reasonable for you to doubt that he would win the lottery, based on the probabilities involved.

Imagine, however, that Alex calls you on the day of the draw in a state of unprecedented excitement. He's almost hysterical as he screams down the phone, 'I WON THE LOTTERY! I WON THE LOTTERY!' If you've known Alex for many years, and you know that he's a generally level-headed and trustworthy person who's not the least bit given to practical jokes, wouldn't you now have *some* reason to believe that he really had won the lottery? The point here is that the probability that an event has occurred can be *raised* when we have specific evidence for it—in this case, your friend's testimony backed up by his personal trustworthiness.

Still, you could be forgiven for retaining some skepticism. After all, it was a ten-million-to-one shot! So imagine that you immediately go around to Alex's house, and he shows you the lottery ticket he bought, his receipt for the ticket, and the official lottery website with the winning numbers. With your own eyes, you

---

6. It's very important to distinguish 'Alex wins the lottery' from 'Someone wins the lottery'. The second scenario could be quite likely, perhaps even inevitable, depending on the kind of lottery. But we're considering here the first scenario, which would be extremely unlikely, since we're focusing on a specific individual.

can see that the six numbers line up exactly. Would it be reasonable in those circumstances to say to Alex, 'Sorry, I simply refuse to believe it, because the chances of you winning the lottery are just so improbable!' There *could* be alternative explanations. You *could* be the victim of a very elaborate hoax, for example. But in light of all the evidence, it would be perfectly reasonable for you to conclude that your friend had indeed won the lottery. (And now would be the appropriate time to remind him just how *good* a friend he is.)

THE REASONABLENESS OF THE RESURRECTION

I hope you can see that the initial improbability of an event isn't a sufficient reason to think it didn't happen. We have to take into account other factors, such as the context of the event and the specific evidence we have that it actually occurred. Considered entirely in the abstract, with no historical context, someone dying and coming back to life *is* extraordinarily improbable. But clearly Jesus was no ordinary person! If *anyone* could be described as extraordinary, it would be Jesus. He wasn't just a random first-century Jew who had nothing else to distinguish Him. The resurrection wasn't a freak supernatural event that happened out of the blue with no connection to other events. Quite the contrary: the resurrection was the climax of a series of remarkable events that stretched far back into human history.

In the previous chapter I discussed how Jesus explicitly claimed to be the Messiah, a savior-king sent from God in fulfilment of numerous Old Testament prophecies. Some of these prophecies, such as Isaiah 53, indicated that the Messiah would suffer and die to make atonement for sin. But other prophecies implied that this Messiah would also be raised from the dead. One is particularly striking:

> You will not abandon me to the realm of the dead,
> nor will you let your faithful one see decay.[7]

As Jesus' disciples later pointed out, although this was written by the Israelite king David a thousand years before Jesus was born, it couldn't apply to David himself because David died and his body *did* decay.[8] It was pointing forward to one who would die, but not stay dead.

Jesus Himself confirmed this expectation by explicitly predicting on several occasions not only that He would be put to death because of His claims, but also that He would rise from the dead.[9] There's no doubt that Jesus was absolutely serious and sincere when He made these predictions. Admittedly, the fact that Jesus predicted His resurrection doesn't prove that the resurrection occurred.

---

7. Psalm 16:10.

8. Acts 2:22-32; 13:34-37.

9. Mark 8:31; 9:9; 9:31; 10:34.

But when we put those predictions in the context of everything else Jesus said and did—His remarkable teachings, His superlative moral character, and His reputation as a miracle-worker—it should at least raise our expectations.

The fact that Jesus was renowned as a healer and a miracle-worker, even among His enemies, is particularly significant here. To repeat: Jesus was clearly no ordinary man. Even secular historians will concede that Jesus had a well-established reputation as a miraculous healer, an exorcist with supernatural power over evil spirits, and one who possessed the power even to raise the dead (although those historians disagree about *how* Jesus gained that reputation). Everything we know about Jesus heightens the expectation that His predictions about His own death would come true.

In addition to all this, there is the solid eyewitness testimony, preserved in the New Testament, that Jesus didn't stay dead. Jesus wasn't buried in an unmarked grave, but in an easily identifiable stone tomb owned by a well-known public figure.[10] A stone was rolled in front of the tomb and a guard posted outside it precisely because of Jesus' own predictions. The authorities who had Jesus killed didn't believe for a moment that He

---

10. Matthew 27:57-60; Mark 15:42-46; Luke 23:50-53; John 19:38-42.

would rise from the dead, but they wanted to ensure that none of His followers would try to fake a resurrection!

Despite these precautions, when some of Jesus' most devoted followers visited His tomb on the Sunday after His crucifixion they discovered that the tomb was open and there was nobody inside—or rather, there was no *body* inside. The only trace of Him were the burial cloths in which He had been wrapped. In the weeks that followed, Jesus' disciples had many encounters which they were absolutely convinced were real meetings with Jesus, physically risen from the dead. It's important to recognize that these weren't fleeting, ghostly apparitions. The disciples talked with Jesus. They ate with Him. They touched Him. They had every opportunity to confirm that they weren't hallucinating or seeing a ghost.

It's just as important to note that some of the people who testified about seeing Jesus alive weren't believers before His crucifixion. One of them was Jesus' half-brother, James. Before Jesus' death, James was a skeptic, but soon afterwards he became a leader in the fledgling Christian church.[11] What could have changed his mind?

Another very significant witness is the apostle Paul. His testimony is particularly weighty because he's an *independent* witness with no prior reason to accept the

---

11. Matthew 13:55; Mark 3:31-35; John 7:1-10; Acts 1:14; 15:13; 21:17-18.

resurrection. In fact, he initially persecuted the first converts to Christianity.[12] But out of the blue, according to his own testimony, he had a direct supernatural encounter with Jesus that turned his life around 180 degrees. He was transformed from a persecutor of Christians into a preacher of Christianity and a persecuted Christian himself. What could account for that?

The combined strength of all the eyewitness testimony to Jesus' resurrection is quite remarkable. This wasn't just one or two disciples trying to salvage their master's reputation, seeing how far they could get away with it. No, hundreds of people from diverse backgrounds, some of whom were initially skeptical and hostile, claimed to have met Jesus alive after His crucifixion on multiple occasions. Many of them were ready to die rather than renounce their testimonies. It defies reason to think they were all either lying or deceived.

So in addition to the prior expectation of Jesus' resurrection, there is substantial credible testimonial evidence that He was raised to life again after His crucifixion. And all of this fits neatly into the broader context of the Christian worldview. The resurrection of Jesus isn't some kind of 'super-duper-miracle' just

---

12. Acts 8:1-3; 9:1-9; Philippians 3:6; 1 Timothy 1:13.

thrown into the Christian worldview to make it a bit more exciting, like extra spice tossed into a soup. It's an integral part of the biblical storyline. Death is the just punishment for our rebellion against God and our inhumanity towards others. The mission of the Messiah was to make atonement for our sin and to restore us to a right relationship with God. This atonement would therefore have to deal with both the guilt of sin and the consequences of sin, including death. How could Jesus claim to conquer death for us while being defeated by death Himself? How could Jesus offer other people eternal life unless He demonstrated that He could live forever?

In one sense, Jesus' resurrection is the confirmation that He really was who He claimed to be and that He really did what He came to do. If Jesus' claim to be equal with God was *false*—and therefore blasphemous—would God have raised Him from the dead? On the other hand, if Jesus was indeed the divine Son of God, we would hardly expect Him *not* to be raised from the dead! If He had stayed dead, a question mark would hang over His entire mission. Did His atoning sacrifice actually work? Was it acceptable to God? The resurrection serves as the divine stamp of approval on Jesus' entire mission.

In sum, Christianity *without* the resurrection of Jesus would make little sense. So to the extent that we have reason to believe the other elements of the Christian worldview—and I've argued that we do—we also have reason to believe in the resurrection. Like those 'Puzzle Balls' I mentioned in chapter 2, the Christian worldview locks together as an integrated whole.

THE UNREASONABLENESS OF THE ALTERNATIVES

But perhaps you still have your doubts. If so, that's not unexpected. If you're resistant to other elements of the Christian worldview, you'll also be doubtful about this central element of the Christian worldview, simply because of the integrated nature of worldviews. Odd as it may sound, such resistance is actually consistent with the teachings of Christianity. One of the teachings of the Bible is that faith in Jesus Christ has to be supernaturally given because of the effects of sin on our hearts and minds. No matter how reasonable Christian beliefs may be, they don't come naturally, because by nature we don't want to accept that we're sinners under God's judgment and there's nothing we can do to save ourselves.

Nevertheless, as you digest what I've said in this chapter I want to encourage you to ask this simple question: *What's the alternative?*

The Christian worldview offers a coherent picture of the identity and mission of Jesus. It accounts for all the historical documentary evidence we possess about Jesus' life and the events that followed His crucifixion.

So if Jesus didn't actually rise from the dead, what on earth *did* happen? What alternative explanation can adequately account for the testimonies recorded in the New Testament and the historical origins of the Christian church?

People who reject the resurrection of Jesus typically do so because they're resistant to the very idea of the supernatural. So they'll try to come up with *naturalistic* alternatives. The trouble is that these alternatives don't make much sense even on their own terms.

Let's run through several of these alternatives to illustrate the point. Some people have suggested that Jesus didn't actually die on the cross; He just passed out and regained consciousness in the tomb. Somehow He then managed to escape from the tomb and persuaded His disciples that He'd risen from the dead. Frankly, this theory has more holes than a mole-infested golf course. If the Romans knew anything at all, they knew how to execute people. It's incredible to think that Jesus could not only have survived a crucifixion, but also have recovered sufficiently from His injuries to wriggle out of His burial wrappings, push away the stone from the tomb, overcome the guards, and then persuade His disciples He'd been raised from the dead by the power of God. (Just imagine the scene: 'Look, God raised me from the dead! Now quit staring and get me to a hospital!')

Others have suggested that Jesus' own disciples stole His body from the tomb and faked His resurrection: the whole thing was a gigantic hoax. But like other conspiracy theories, this proposal is more concerned with explaining away the evidence than with following it, and it raises far more questions than it answers. We have to ask what the disciples would have to gain from such a deception. Why would they be willing to suffer persecution, even death, for claims they knew full well to be *false*? How plausible is it that *everyone* would go along with such a massive con—that not a single disciple would break ranks and blow the whistle? And what about those late converts, like James and Paul, who weren't believers before the crucifixion yet claimed also to have seen Jesus alive?

Another theory is that Jesus' body was removed by the Jewish or Roman authorities. But this suggestion makes little sense. What reason would they have for doing that? Why would they protect the tomb with a stone and a guard and then remove the body *themselves*? Even if they had moved the body somewhere else, surely they would have whipped it out as soon as the disciples started claiming that Jesus had risen from the dead and put an end to the story. Furthermore, this proposal doesn't begin to explain all the appearances of Jesus which the disciples experienced. No one would have been convinced of Jesus' resurrection solely on the basis of a missing body.

Perhaps the most popular explanation offered by skeptics is the 'hallucination theory', according to which the appearances of Jesus were really just hallucinations experienced by the disciples. Yet there are multiple problems with this hypothesis too. Hallucinations are by nature subjective and individual. There's no scientific basis for the idea that a group of people can have the same hallucination simultaneously and on repeated occasions. Furthermore, hallucinations tend to align with a person's expectations, but many of the first believers didn't *expect* Jesus to be resurrected. (The apostle Paul certainly didn't.) Studies have also shown that hallucinations rarely lead people to make major life-changes. So the hallucination theory doesn't offer a reasonable explanation for the testimonies and actions of the first Christians. Nor does it begin to explain what happened to Jesus' body. ('Hey guys, do you think we should maybe check the tomb?')

There are other naturalistic theories, but the point has been made. In the end there has to be *some* satisfactory explanation for the remarkable events that took place after Jesus' crucifixion. If Jesus didn't rise from the dead—if His bones are still buried somewhere outside Jerusalem—then what's your alternative explanation for those events?

If you accept that God *could* have raised Jesus to life again, I suggest to you that there's no better explanation for the evidence. I'm confident that if you think through the alternatives you'll see that all of them come apart when closely scrutinized. The only serious objection to the idea that Jesus rose from the dead is the objection that *miracles just don't happen*—which is tantamount to denying God's existence. But if we deny God's existence, we can't make sense of *anything* in this world, never mind the historical origins of Christianity.

So why should you believe in the resurrection of Jesus? For two basic reasons. First, the resurrection of Jesus is an integral element of the Christian worldview, and only the Christian worldview makes sense of the things we take for granted about the universe and our place in it. Secondly, only the resurrection of Jesus makes sense of what we know about the life of Jesus, the lives of His earliest followers, the writings of the New Testament and the origins of the Christian church.

8

What Now?

In this relatively short book I've tried to make a positive case for believing Christianity; that is, for believing that the central claims of Christianity are *true*. In this closing chapter I want to try to draw all the threads together and summarize my case in a few pages.

Why should we believe anything at all? Put simply, we should believe something if we have good *reasons* to believe that it is *true*. I've argued that there are many good reasons to believe that Christianity is true. But in order to appreciate those reasons we have to recognize that Christianity is an entire *worldview*: a comprehensive perspective on the universe and our place in it. Everyone has a worldview, whether they realize it or not. In the final analysis, only one worldview can be *true*. Only one worldview will give us a *right* view of the world. Only one worldview fits reality—and that's the worldview we should believe.

I discussed several criteria for evaluating worldviews, so we can determine *which* worldview is the most reasonable one. For any worldview we're assessing, we can ask these questions:

- Is the worldview self-contradictory or self-refuting?

- Does it cohere well—that is, do its various tenets fit together and support one another?

- Can it account for the things we take for granted in our experience of the world and in our everyday lives?

- Does it make good sense of the available evidence?

My contention is that when we apply these criteria to the major worldviews held by people today, the Christian worldview is in a class of its own.

In chapter 4 I argued that many of the things we take for granted in life make sense only if there is a transcendent, personal God who created and sustains the universe.

In chapter 5 I made the case for Christianity's claim that the Bible is God's Word to us. If there is a God, He would *speak* to us. He would communicate with us using language, so that we can enjoy a personal relationship with Him. And when we consider the various candidates for a divine revelation, nothing comes close to the Bible.

In chapter 6 we explored another worldview-defining issue: the true identity of Jesus of Nazareth. I explained how His astonishing claim to be the promised Messiah and the divine Son of God fits into the broader Christian worldview, and how Jesus demonstrated that His claim was no empty boast.

In chapter 7 we considered another distinctive tenet of the Christian worldview: the claim that God raised Jesus from the dead. I explained why this tenet is an integral element of the Christian worldview, why objections to miracles implicitly deny the existence of God, and why it's reasonable to believe that Jesus really did rise again from the dead, just as He said he would.

So here's the bottom line. Only a worldview that is centered on an absolute, personal God can account for the most basic features of this universe, such as its existence and orderliness, and the most basic features of human experience, such as self-consciousness, reason and moral values. When we examine the main contenders for God-centered worldviews, we can see that the Christian worldview is really the only coherent and viable one. No other worldview comes close to the Christian worldview. No other religion's scriptures come close to the Bible in their credibility. No other religious figure's teachings and deeds come close to those of Jesus.

But What About …?

There are several things I *haven't* done in this book. For one thing, although I've given many reasons why you should believe Christianity, I haven't explained why you *shouldn't* believe some *other* religion or worldview—at least, I haven't done that directly. In order to keep this book focused and relatively concise, I haven't discussed in any detail the other major religions and worldviews out there. Nevertheless, by making a positive case for Christianity, I've *indirectly* explained why its competitors fall short.

For example, I argued in chapter 4 that our worldview needs to be centered on a God who is both absolute and personal. That rules out atheistic worldviews, of course, but also many religious worldviews that don't acknowledge an absolute, personal God. Religions denying such a God include Buddhism, Taoism, Mormonism and most forms of Hinduism. In addition, I explained in chapter 5 why we should believe that God has spoken to us, specifically in the Bible. If I'm right, that rules out worldviews such as Deism which affirm some kind of divine architect, but deny that this deity wants to relate to us personally through verbal communication.

It also rules out worldviews with scriptures that conflict with the Bible. Chapters 6 and 7 made the case for two central tenets of Christianity: Jesus was the divine Son of God, and Jesus rose from the dead. If those tenets are true, all non-Christian religions and ideologies have to be rejected. So although I haven't explicitly discussed all the alternatives to Christianity, they're at least addressed indirectly by my arguments.

Another thing I haven't done is to respond to common objections and arguments *against* Christianity, such as these:

- What about all the evil and suffering in the world? Doesn't that disprove the existence of an all-good, all-powerful God?

- What about the Big Bang and the Darwinian theory of evolution? Hasn't modern science shown that we don't need a Creator after all?

- Aren't there errors and contradictions in the Bible? Wouldn't that prove it isn't divinely inspired after all?

- Why does God appear so mean and vindictive in the Old Testament? How do Christians reconcile that with the teachings of Jesus?

- How could an all-loving God send anyone to hell?

- If Christianity is so great, why do some Christians behave so poorly?

Perhaps you've had some of these objections in your mind the whole time you've been reading this book, and you've been wondering, 'When will he get around to addressing these?' If so, I'm sorry to disappoint you! But as I mentioned above, my aim has been to keep this book to a respectable length and to focus specifically on the *positive* reasons for believing Christianity. Each of the objections above deserves to be addressed in more detail. In fact, each one deserves an entire book devoted to it—which is precisely why this book is part of a larger series. Other titles in the series will deal with some of the common objections to Christianity.

That said, I don't want to give the impression that I'm trying to dodge these issues. So let me at least say the following in response. As I've considered the various objections people raise against Christianity, they typically fall into two basic categories. In the first category there are objections that simply miss the target because they're based on a misunderstanding or misrepresentation of what Christianity actually teaches. So the objections attack a 'straw man': they're really objections to a poor imposter rather than the genuine article.

In the second category there are criticisms which are directed at Christianity but tacitly take for granted some *other* worldview than the Christian one. For example, many people object to Christianity's teachings on sexual ethics, but that's precisely because they're getting their views on morality from a non-Christian worldview in the first place. They hold fundamentally different assumptions about God and His purposes for us than those Christians hold. But in that case, their objections simply *presuppose* that Christianity is wrong. It's hardly a compelling objection to say you reject Christianity because it's not something *other* than Christianity.

A further irony is that many of the common objections to Christianity also unwittingly *depend* on the Christian worldview. For example, moral objections and scientific objections hold water only if objective moral values are real and scientific knowledge is possible. But as I've argued, both morality and science depend on the existence of God, and the Christian worldview is the only defensible God-centered worldview. Indeed, any suggestion that some non-Christian worldview is 'more reasonable' than Christianity ought to prompt a deeper question: How does that worldview account for reason itself?

So while I haven't directly addressed the various common objections to Christianity, what I have argued in this book still goes some way toward indicating where many of these objections go wrong.

What's the Alternative?

Perhaps you're not persuaded by the case I've offered. Perhaps you don't think there are enough reasons—or enough *good* reasons—to believe that Christianity is true. If so, let me say that I'm thankful you've taken the time to read this book and I appreciate the fact that you're willing to think through the issues. But let me leave you with this one question to ponder:

What's the alternative?

If Christianity isn't true, then what *is* true?

As I've emphasized in this book, everyone has a worldview. Everyone *needs* a worldview in order to interpret the world and try to make sense of it. In the end, only one worldview can be true, because different worldviews make conflicting truth-claims. Furthermore, some worldview or other *must* be true. There must be *some* worldview that ultimately makes sense of the world. There must be *some* worldview that's coherent and 'fits' reality. If it isn't the Christian worldview, which worldview is it? Which worldview is *more reasonable* to believe than the biblical one? The question cannot be avoided.

Let me press home the point with an analogy. Suppose a murder has been committed: a body has been found in the woods, riddled with stab wounds. It's obvious that the victim didn't die of natural causes! One of the main suspects, we'll suppose, is a work colleague of the victim named Ivan Ife. Ivan appears to have had both motive and opportunity. However, after evaluating all the evidence the detective investigating the case has some lingering doubts and finds that he can't believe that Ivan actually committed the crime. Does that mean the case is closed?

Of course not! *Somebody* murdered the victim. If the murderer wasn't Ivan, it had to be someone else. So the question must be asked: If it wasn't Ivan, *then who was it?* What's the alternative theory? There has to be *some* truth about who committed the crime. Even if 'Ivan Ife' is the wrong answer, there still has to be a *right* answer.

In the same way, if you think Christianity is the wrong answer to the question of which worldview makes sense of the world, there still has to be a right answer. So what is your answer? And how would you go about defending it?

You might be tempted to turn my analogy back on me. 'Sometimes crimes never get solved. If there's not enough evidence to convict any of the suspects, we have to suspend judgment. We can't reach any conclusion about whodunnit.' Granted, sometimes the police have to take that stance with respect to the perpetrator of a crime. The problem is, none of us can take that stance with respect to our worldview. We cannot function at all without *some* worldview—we have to stand somewhere. Even if you don't want to stand in one particular place, you can't stand *nowhere*.

So the question still seems unavoidable. We have to consider *which* worldview is the right one. If not the Christian worldview, which is it?

What's the alternative?

GOD STILL SPEAKS

I hope I've gone some way in this book toward persuading you that you should believe Christianity. But if you're not convinced—at least, not yet!—I won't be too shocked. In the first place, it's challenging to step outside the worldview you already have and see the world from a different perspective. Your worldview influences how you interpret and evaluate facts, evidences and truth-claims. It profoundly shapes what you think is reasonable, plausible and possible. If Christianity looks unreasonable to you, that's very likely because you're judging it through the lens of your current worldview rather than considering it on its own terms. In effect, I'm asking you to 'take off' your current worldview—just for the sake of argument—and to 'try on' the Christian worldview. I'm inviting you to try to see the world through a *different* lens. But that's a challenging thing to do.

What's more, if Christianity really is true then something quite paradoxical follows: it's *reasonable* to believe in Christianity, but it's not *natural* to believe it. That's because, as Christianity teaches, all of us are born corrupted by sin and in a state of rebellion against God. Sin distorts how we see the world and disrupts our relationship with God. It causes our rebellious desires to interfere with our God-given reason. It clouds our judgment. It makes the reasonable seem unreasonable, and the unreasonable seem reasonable. Sin is a kind of deep-rooted irrationality that we can't simply shake off by sheer force of will or by trying to reason our way out of it.

We need outside assistance. Indeed, we need *supernatural* assistance. That's precisely why Christianity teaches that a supernatural work of God is required in a person's heart and mind in order for them to accept the Christian faith. For that acceptance demands nothing less than a personal trust in Jesus Christ as Lord and Savior—and thus a wholesale transfer of allegiance.

Perhaps you're thinking, if it takes a supernatural work of God to believe in Christianity, wasn't it a waste of time to write this book? No, not at all. The fact is that God normally uses *human means* to accomplish His purposes. Take the Bible, for example. I suppose God *could* have dropped the Bible down from heaven on golden plates. But instead he used human authors to write it, under the guidance of the Holy Spirit. Likewise, God *could* have sent angels around the world to tell people about Jesus. But instead He used Jesus' own disciples for the task—and He's still using Jesus' followers today to accomplish that purpose.

In a similar way then, God may be pleased to use this book to accomplish His purpose of bringing about an entire reorientation of someone's life.

For all I know, God is doing that right now, at this very moment. So let me leave you with a final thought. One of the points I've emphasized in this book is that God is real and He *speaks* to us. Not only has God spoken in the past, He *continues* to speak to people today—and that includes you.

God speaks through His creation, through the natural order.

God speaks through the human conscience, pressing upon us an awareness of His moral laws and our guiltiness in breaking them.

God speaks through His inspired scriptures, the Bible.

Above all, God speaks through Jesus, whose teachings and deeds have been faithfully recorded and preserved through the centuries so that we can know Him, trust Him and love Him.

God is speaking.

Are you listening?

Do you hear God speaking to you?

If you're beginning to think that there *are* good reasons to believe in Christianity after all—if the

Christian worldview is actually starting to make more sense to you—then I humbly suggest that may be the sign of a supernatural work in you. It's an indication that God is giving you eyes to see the world as He meant you to see it. Even more importantly, it's a sign that God is giving you ears to hear the message He wants you to hear—the truly astounding message that because of God's immeasurable love, rebels like us can have the slate wiped clean and receive eternal life through His Son, Jesus Christ.

> For God so loved the world that he gave his one and only Son, that whoever believes in him shall not perish but have eternal life.[1]

> God demonstrates his own love for us in this: While we were still sinners, Christ died for us.[2]

> This is love: not that we loved God, but that he loved us and sent his Son as an atoning sacrifice for our sins.[3]

> If you declare with your mouth, 'Jesus is Lord', and believe in your heart that God raised him from the dead, you will be saved.[4]

---

1. John 3:16.
2. Romans 5:8.
3. 1 John 4:10.
4. Romans 10:9.

Suggested Further Reading

T. D. Alexander, *The Servant King: The Bible's Portrait of the Messiah* (InterVarsity Press, 1998). This introductory book explains how the idea of God's promised Messiah, a servant-king who would bring salvation to God's people, is developed in the Old Testament and was fulfilled by Jesus in the New Testament. For a deeper treatment: Herbert W. Bateman IV, Darrell L. Bock and Gordon H. Johnston, *Jesus the Messiah* (Kregel Academic, 2012).

Robert M. Bowman, Jr. and J. Ed Komoszewski, *Putting Jesus in His Place: The Case for the Deity of Christ* (Kregel, 2007). The authors present a multifaceted case that the New Testament consistently teaches the full divinity of Jesus, thereby demonstrating that belief in Jesus' divinity wasn't a late development in the Christian church.

Stewart Goetz and Charles Taliaferro, *Naturalism* (Eerdmans, 2008). This short but scholarly book elaborates on some of the arguments I offered in chapter 4, i.e. that Naturalism cannot account for basic features of human experience such as reason and consciousness.

Guillermo Gonzales and Jay W. Richards, *The Privileged Planet* (Regnery, 2004). The authors (an astronomer and a philosopher) explain why our planet is not only fine-tuned to support life but also specially situated to enable scientific investigation of the universe.

Craig S. Keener, *Miracles: The Credibility of the New Testament Accounts* (Baker Academic, 2011). A mammoth two-volume defense of the credibility of the miracle claims in the New Testament. Very comprehensive and scholarly, with detailed responses to all the common arguments against miracles.

John C. Lennox, *God's Undertaker: Has Science Buried God?* (Lion Hudson, 2007). An engaging book by a University of Oxford professor who argues that modern science supports belief in God rather than undermining it. If you want to go deeper, check out the two books by Stephen Meyer mentioned in the footnotes of chapter 4.

Victor Reppert, *C. S. Lewis's Dangerous Idea: In Defense of the Argument from Reason* (InterVarsity Press, 2003).

This book develops in more detail one of the arguments I gave in chapter 4, namely, that our very ability to reason points us to God.

Mark D. Roberts, *Can We Trust the Gospels?* (Crossway, 2007). The author, a New Testament scholar, explains in a very accessible way why the four Gospels should be treated as reliable historical accounts based on eye-witness testimony.

John R. W. Stott, *The Cross of Christ* (InterVarsity Press, 2006). A classic exposition of the Christian teaching that Jesus died as an atoning sacrifice to bring about our salvation. Answers the questions, 'Why did Jesus have to die?' and 'What difference does it make?'

John Wenham, *Christ and the Bible*, 3rd ed. (Wipf & Stock, 2009). Christians claim to follow the teachings of Christ, so it's important to know what Jesus Himself believed and taught about the Bible. Wenham's book answers that crucial question clearly and thoroughly.

James R. White, *The Forgotten Trinity* (Bethany House, 1998). One of the clearest expositions of the Christian doctrine of the Trinity and its basis in the Bible.

James R. White, *What Every Christian Needs to Know About the Qur'an* (Bethany House, 2013). This book discusses in more detail one of the points I made in chapter 5, that the Quran (the holy book of Islam) undermines its own credibility as a divine revelation by what it claims about Christianity and the Bible.

The Big Ten
Critical Questions Answered

This is a Christian apologetics series which aims to address ten commonly asked questions about God, the Bible, and Christianity. Each book, while easy to read, is challenging and thought-provoking, addressing subjects ranging from hell to science. A good read whatever your present opinions.

The books in this series are:

THE BIG TEN
critical questions answered

SERIES EDITORS
James N. Anderson and Greg Welty

Does Christianity Really Work?

William Edgar

ISBN 978-1-78191-775-6

Does Christianity Really Work?

WILLIAM EDGAR

Wasn't the South African Apartheid supported by Christians? Weren't the Crusades motivated by greed, but advocated by the church? Don't phoney television preachers manipulate viewers into donating money? William Edgar addresses these and other questions honestly, without attempting to dismiss or explain away their uncomfortable realities. He displays the good aspects of the church even more brilliantly through frankly and Biblically acknowledging the bad. If you have ever asked the question Does Christianity Really Work? this will be an interesting and enlightening read, whatever your prior convictions.

... addresses one of the main questions that sceptics and seekers have about Christianity - does it actually work? Looking at some issues from a positive perspective (the good that Christianity has done, and continues to do) and others from a negative (the alleged harm it is supposed to have brought), Edgar gives reasoned, evidenced and clear answers. This is a good primer for the seeker or the sceptic.

David Robertson
Pastor, St Peter's Free Church of Scotland, Dundee & trustee of
SOLAS, Centre for Public Christianity

William Edgar is Professor of Apologetics at Westminister Theological Seminary in Philadelphia, and an accomplished jazz pianist. He is married to Barbara and they have two children, William and Deborah.

THE DAWKINS LETTERS
CHALLENGING ATHEIST MYTHS   **DAVID ROBERTSON**

ISBN 978-1-84550-597-4

The Dawkins Letters

Challenging Atheist Myths

DAVID ROBERTSON

When Richard Dawkins published *The God Delusion*, David Robertson wanted an intelligent Christian response – and so he wrote it. This honest book draws on Robertson's experience as a debater, letter writer, pastor and author to clarify the questions and the answers for thinkers and seekers, and to respond to Dawkins in a gentle spirit.

The book does a particularly good job of point out the unending contradictions between what Dawkins wants to believe and what he must actually believe.

Tim Challies
Blogger at www.challies.com

The content is excellent. It's a fun, engaging read.

Ligon Duncan
Chancellor and CEO, Reformed Theological Seminary

Wow, this is an intelligent and well-crafted view of RD's book.
Response from an atheist on Richard Dawkins Website

David Robertson is pastor of St Peter's Free Church of Scotland in Dundee, Scotland. Robertson is a trustee of the Solas Centre for Public Christianity and works to fulfil the Centre's mission to engage culture with the message of Christ.

MAGNIFICENT
OBSESSION
WHY JESUS *IS* GREAT
DAVID ROBERTSON

ISBN 978-1-78191-271-3

Magnificent Obsession

Why Jesus is *Great*

David Robertson

David Robertson was told by the leader of an atheist society: "Okay, I admit that you have destroyed my atheism, but what do you believe?" His answer was "I believe in and because of Jesus." This book shows us why Jesus is the reason to believe. In response to the shout of "God is not Great" by the late Christopher Hitchens, David shows us why Jesus is God and is Great.

Engaging and insightful... This book is useful no matter what your experience and where you stand on matters of faith.

Tim Keller
Senior Pastor, Redeemer Presbyterian Church
New York City, New York

We will share this 'Magnificent Obsession' so that ... friends may discover not only what it means but why it matters.

Alistair Begg
Senior Pastor, Parkside Church, Chagrin Falls, Ohio

I love this book! It's an excellent, conversational introduction to Christianity for non-Christians and new Christians who are wrestling with questions.

Jon Bloom
President, Desiring God, Minneapolis, Minnesota

David and I disagree on a great many things, but we are unified understanding the importance of this ongoing debate.

Gary McLelland
Atheist, blogger and secular campaigner, Edinburgh, Scotland

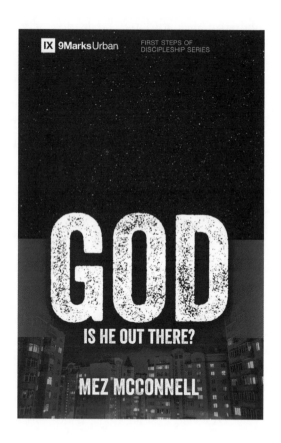

GOD

IS HE OUT THERE?

MEZ MCCONNELL

ISBN 978-1-78191-710-7

God

Is He Out There?

Mez McConnell

If God exists, prove it then? If God exists, what does it have to do with me? If all this is true, now what?

This series of short workbooks, from the 9 Marks Urban series, are designed to help you think through some of life's big questions. It all starts with the most important question of all: God-Is He Out There? The questions that follow all hinge on our answer to that question. If we answer that there is a God, then how can we get to know Him and how should we now live?

... brilliantly simple and accessible to anyone searching for answers about God and truth, and yet biblically sound and clear about what it truly means to know Christ and walk with him. Mez has a sensitive pastor's heart and a burden for the urban poor that oozes with every page. This book is a clear and needed contribution from one of the most careful and wise thinkers on caring for the poor in our generation.

Brian Croft
Pastor, Auburndale Baptist Church, Louisville, Kentucky &
Founder of Practical Shepherding

God – Is He out There? *is a clear explanation of what God says about himself without talking down to people. It's a great opportunity to think about the most important questions of all: Does God exist? What's he like? And what's it got to do with me?*

Tim Chester
Pastor of Grace Church, Boroughbridge, Yorkshire

Mez McConnell is the pastor for Niddrie Community Church, near Edinburgh. He is also the Director of 20schemes which is dedicated to revitalising and planting gospel churches in Scotland's poorest communities. Previously he was a missionary with street kids in Brazil. He is married and has two children.

Christian Focus Publications

Our mission statement –

STAYING FAITHFUL

In dependence upon God we seek to impact the world through literature faithful to His infallible Word, the Bible. Our aim is to ensure that the Lord Jesus Christ is presented as the only hope to obtain forgiveness of sin, live a useful life and look forward to heaven with Him.

Our books are published in four imprints:

CHRISTIAN
FOCUS

Popular works including biographies, commentaries, basic doctrine and Christian living.

CHRISTIAN
HERITAGE

Books representing some of the best material from the rich heritage of the church.

MENTOR

Books written at a level suitable for Bible College and seminary students, pastors, and other serious readers. The imprint includes commentaries, doctrinal studies, examination of current issues and church history.

CF4•K

Children's books for quality Bible teaching and for all age groups: Sunday school curriculum, puzzle and activity books; personal and family devotional titles, biographies and inspirational stories – because you are never too young to know Jesus!

Christian Focus Publications Ltd,
Geanies House, Fearn, Ross-shire,
IV20 1TW, Scotland, United Kingdom.
www.christianfocus.com